Why They Can't Write

Why They Can't Write

*Killing the Five-Paragraph Essay
and Other Necessities*

JOHN WARNER

Johns Hopkins University Press   *Baltimore*

Johns Hopkins University Press
2715 North Charles Street
Baltimore, Maryland 21218-4363
www.press.jhu.edu

Library of Congress Cataloging-in-Publication Data

Names: Warner, John, 1970– author.
Title: Why they can't write : killing the five-paragraph essay and other
    necessities / John Warner.
Description: Baltimore : Johns Hopkins University Press, 2018. |
    Includes bibliographical references and index.
Identifiers: LCCN 2018013348 | ISBN 9781421427102 (hardcover :
    acid-free paper) | ISBN 9781421427119 (electronic) | ISBN
    1421427109 (hardcover : acid-free paper) | ISBN 1421427117
    (electronic)
Subjects: LCSH: English language—Composition and exercises—
    Study and teaching—United States. | English language—
    Rhetoric—Study and teaching—United States. | Critical
    thinking—Study and teaching—United States.
Classification: LCC LB1576 .W2596 2019 | DDC 808/.042071—dc23
    LC record available at https://lccn.loc.gov/2018013348

A catalog record for this book is available from the British Library.

Special discounts are available for bulk purchases of this book.
For more information, please contact Special Sales at 410-516-6936 or
specialsales@press.jhu.edu.

Johns Hopkins University Press uses environmentally friendly book
materials, including recycled text paper that is composed of at least
30 percent post-consumer waste, whenever possible.

For my teachers at Greenbriar School (1975–1982),
from your grateful student

Contents

PART FOUR
UNANSWERED QUESTIONS

Why They Can't Write

Our Writing "Crisis"

There seems to be widespread agreement that when it comes to the writing skills of college students, and even recent college graduates, we are in the midst of a crisis.

I have twenty years of experience teaching writing at the college level. Despite my best efforts, people sometimes discover this fact, and when they do, they ask: *Why can't my new employees write?*

I ask my new friends what they mean when they say this. My new friends shake their heads like a fly is buzzing around their faces as they wave their hands in annoyance. *What they write doesn't make sense! I can't even understand the sentences, let alone the message! I have to redo everything! And why do they keep saying "plethora"?*

We're often talking about young people of significant promise, graduates of highly selective universities. Some of them even have postgraduate degrees in law or business. They are supposed to be better than whatever it is they are.

"Why do *you* think they can't write?" I ask.

They guess that the current generation is somehow defective—coddled snowflakes who have never been properly challenged.

"So, lack of rigor," I say.

Exactly!

"It's not lack of rigor," I say. At least it's not lack of rigor in the ways they're thinking about the term. They look doubtful, but for the moment they are willing to defer to my alleged expertise.

So, it's the cell phones . . . that makes sense. We should get a time machine and destroy the damn things.

Sometimes they say this while simultaneously looking at their phones.

"It's not the cell phones, either," I say.

Their faces now look fully skeptical, side-eye city. They're wondering if, despite my credentials—not just the many years in the college writing classroom, but also a parallel career as a writer and editor—I might not know what I'm talking about. Maybe *I'm* the problem, a bad teacher who won't hold students accountable.

I am partly to blame, no doubt, but the fault isn't in bad students or bad teachers. I turn to my new friends, wondering if they're ready for the truth. Willing to give me one more chance to prove I'm not a lost cause, they ask one more time.

What is it then?

"They're doing exactly what we've trained them to do; that's the problem."

The Danger of Training Wheels

I was upset one recent morning after clicking a Facebook link and seeing that generations of American children were taught, incorrectly, how to ride a bike.

I am one of them.

At first the training wheels were a gift, allowing me to range freely throughout the neighborhood and even ride my red-, white-, and blue-streamered Schwinn Pixie in the 1976 bicentennial Fourth of July parade. I was six that summer, which is plenty old enough to ride without training wheels, but why bother to learn how to ride a bike without training wheels when the training wheels don't actually keep you from doing what you want to do anyway?

As I turned seven and headed toward eight, though, things started to change. For one, I became the last kid still tooling around with training wheels, a juicy target for bullies. For another, I had set my eye on a red Schwinn Stingray with a banana seat, but I knew the bike's cool factor would drop considerably with the addition of training wheels.

When I show my students pictures of the Stingray, they have a hard time believing it was once an object of deep desire. The heart wants what it wants, though, and I wanted a Stingray. So, finally needing to learn to ride without training wheels, I engaged in the time-honored tradition of pedaling away while my father ran alongside, holding me steady until I was off on my own.

In theory, it was the training wheels that allowed me to ride freely without help not long after my father released his grip and yelled at me to "pedal, pedal, pedal." In reality, we've learned over the intervening years that those training wheels were far more hindrance than help when it came to learning to ride a bike.

The reason? Training wheels actually *prevent* young riders from practicing the most important skill for riding a bike: balance. For sure, training wheels make it safer for kids who don't know how to ride a bike, but when it comes time to ride for real, they haven't spent quality, focused time on that much more essential skill.[1]

Now, just about every expert recommends that kids as young as two start on "balance bikes," pedal-less bikes where the child's feet touch the ground and they propel themselves like they're walking or running. The focus from the beginning is on the key underlying skill that allows for the development of the bigger, more complicated, more important skill.

When it comes to teaching writing, we've been doing something similar, giving students training wheels that actively work against their ability to learn how to write.

The worst of those training wheels is the five-paragraph essay.

If you do not know the form, ask the closest school-aged child or, indeed, anyone who has been through school in the past twenty or so years:

1.   Paragraph of introduction ending in a thesis statement that previews the body paragraphs.

2–4. Body paragraphs of evidence supporting the thesis.

5.   Conclusion that restates the thesis, almost always starting with, "In conclusion."

You might be thinking that this sounds like good, sound writing. Organized, focused, purposeful. After all, writing has rules, doesn't it? You've got to know the rules in order to break them. I have said this very thing in my teaching career, but I was wrong to say it—because it isn't helpful when it comes to *learning* how to write.

Students arrive in my college first-year writing class well familiar with what they've been told are the rules of good writing, most of which come in the form of prohibitions:

Never use "I" in a sentence.

Never use contractions.

No fewer than three and no more than five sentences per paragraph.

No fewer than five and no more than nine words per sentence.

And on and on . . . When I ask students what they've been told about writing, they can list rule after rule. When I ask them where these rules come from, why these rules are rules, they shrug.

Because the teacher said so.

Sitting before me in their first-year college writing class, my students are ready to get their next set of rules, prepped for the authority figure to describe the circumference and height of the hoop I would like them to jump through, worried because this is college and I may also set the hoop on fire. They're not exactly enthusiastic about it—you should see their "ugh" faces when I even say the words "five-paragraph essay"—but instead of giving them more rules, I introduce them to the skill that is the writing equivalent of balance when it comes to riding a bicycle.

Choice.

To write is to make choices, word by word, sentence by sentence, paragraph by paragraph. Writers choose what they want to write about, whom they want to write to, and why they're writing.

For example, I am writing this book because my many years of teaching writing have convinced me that we have taken a wrong turn in our collective approach to teaching writing and we show few signs of getting back on a better path. This is my subject.

With this book I want to speak to policy makers, educators, parents of school-aged children, and even students themselves, so we can engage in conversation and collaboration that will meet the needs of our culture and communities. This is my audience.

I am writing this book because writing and teaching writing have been the focus of my day-to-day work for a long time. I'm convinced I have some worthwhile things to say that deserve to be heard and that no one else is saying on a broad scale.[2] Writing a book is a lousy business proposition, and yet I've done it anyway because I *had* to. This is my purpose.

Unfortunately, the way our nation's schoolchildren are taught—and, more importantly, the way their learning is assessed—gives them little experience with making choices in the context of writing. These distortions of what it means to write offer students even less opportunity to write about things that matter to them or to engage with their own passions.

Instead, much of the writing students are asked to do in school is not writing so much as an *imitation* of writing, creating an artifact resembling writing which is not, in fact, the product of a robust, flexible writing process.

This is not the fault of teachers, or parents, or students, but instead is a consequence of a system put into place bit by bit without sufficient thought as to the larger implications. It is our American enthusiasm for believing in solutions that has caused us to lose sight of the real problems. Much of the work to address the achievement gaps among different categories of students is well-meaning, but it has been terribly misguided.

By trying to guide students toward "proficiency" or "competency," we wind up providing them with rules and strictures that cut students off from the most important and meaningful aspects of writing. In order to be judged "proficient," students are coached to create imitations that pass muster on a test a grader may take all of three minutes to read, or even worse, a test that's assessed by a computer algorithm on the lookout for key words and phrases.

The writing need not be accurate or well argued, and it definitely doesn't need to be interesting; it merely needs to seem like something that *could be* accurate and well argued if we actually cared enough to read it closely. We are asking students to write Potemkin essays, fakes designed to pass surface-level muster that are revealed as hollow facades when inspected more closely. Students are more aware of this than anyone else and it colors their attitudes toward writing.

Acting Like an Actor

Imagine an acting school where rather than helping students develop the individual skills of building a performance, students are instead required to learn a series of impressions of genuine actors performing a role. De Niro 101 would cover Travis Bickle and the father in *Meet the Parents*, for example. Meryl Streep's various performances would be 400-level, no doubt. Our aspiring actors would be graded on 45-second snippet imitations, judged on how accurate they are to the standard set in the original performance.

But what happens when our young thespians are tasked with a role they haven't learned how to mimic, a performance that doesn't yet exist?

This is how we teach students to write. Don't be a writer, we tell them, just do some things that make it look like you know how to write. And when in doubt, at least sound smart by using words like *ubiquitous* and *plethora*. If you want to really show off, try *myriad*.

And when students wind up in college in classes like mine and I tell them the game has changed, that in fact it isn't a game at all, students feel like someone has played a cruel trick. Each successive cohort seems less prepared for the challenges of my college-writing class than the last, not because they're getting less intelligent, or don't want to learn, or have been warped by an "everyone-gets-a-trophy" culture, but because they have been incentivized to create imitations rather than the genuine article.

When confronted with a writing assignment, this is how they respond, larded with rules from origins unknown, yet rules that must be important because a teacher who is tasked with preparing them for a high-stakes standardized assessment has told them so.

For example, on the first day of class I ask students to write in response to two questions: (1) Who are you as a writer? and (2) Who do you want to be as a writer? I am asking them to reflect on their experiences, to share what those experiences with writing mean to them, and to consider what role writing might play in their futures.

Ninety percent of the responses focus on *how good* students think they are at writing. Almost no one talks about what they want to say, the types of writing they're interested in, or what kind of writing they may have to do in the future. They do not recall a favorite example of their writing. Very few express ever having enjoyed any act of writing. Often, it seems like they barely understand the questions, because they have no self-concept of themselves as writers. They are "students," and the worth of a student does not come from the self but from the grades assigned by a teacher.

These are voting-age adults who are old enough to go to war, and when asked about writing they have almost nothing to say. For the most part, even though I have taught exclusively at selective (or better) institutions, students express little confidence in their own abilities. Even those who got A's in high school often say they doubt they're good writers, knowing the work they've been producing is something of a confidence game, good enough to fool at a surface level, but not genuinely meaningful, most significantly to themselves.

This distresses me. We say education is meant to turn students into critical thinkers, to help them prepare for the demands of a dynamic and changing workplace. School is to make students "college- and career-ready." We are not doing this when it comes to teaching writing. We are training students to pass standardized assessments, not teaching them how to write.

The good news is we have broad agreement that something must be done, that students are falling increasingly behind whatever it is they're supposed to be ahead of. Unfortunately, most of what we hear from the education reform front— Standards! Accountability! Grit! Computery Things!—will only exacerbate the problems we're already facing because they address surface-level issues.

Doubling down on what's already failing is not a solution.

We need a thorough rethink, starting with a couple of shibboleths that seem hard to shake when it comes to writing.

PART ONE

Killing the Five-Paragraph Essay

Johnny Could Never Write

Depending on whom you talk to, and more importantly what you're looking for, students have always been poor writers.

The December 1975 cover of *Newsweek* declared, "Why Johnny Can't Write," a reference to Rudolf Franz's 1955 book, *Why Johnny Can't Read*. The story itself discusses the many shortcomings of Johnny's schools and teachers and the quality of instruction.

Newsweek was not particularly timely, though. Almost a hundred years earlier (1878), Harvard professor Adams Sherman Hill said, "Everyone who has had much to do with the graduating classes of our best colleges has known men who could not write a letter describing their own commencements without making blunders which would disgrace a boy twelve years old."[1]

I'm sure it goes back further. I imagine a time when Professor Og was rending his animal skin in frustration over Student Thak's failure to properly etch the antelope glyph onto the cave wall.

Maybe the story of writing is more complicated than some would like to believe.

Some things we know about writing:

Writing is hard.

Consider the different cognitive processes at work when we're trying to write. When we write we are using our long-term memory as we search for knowledge and information. We are using our short-term memory as the sentence unfolds on the page, trying to track what came before and what came next.

We are simultaneously juggling what we want to say with how we want to say it.

Unlike speech, for which we appear to be biologically hardwired, writing requires far more deliberate and focused effort. Even a simple set of directions or a grocery list demands relatively high-level cognitive processing.

In more sophisticated writing, where we're trying to create rather than simply recall knowledge, we're doing one of the most brain-taxing things imaginable.[2]

The more experienced the writer, the more likely they are to articulate the difficulties of writing. Ernest Hemingway said, "We are all apprentices in a craft where no one ever becomes a master."

In *Air & Light & Time & Space: How Successful Academics Write*, Helen Sword looks at the practices and attitudes working academics employ and notes that only a "rare few" find writing "easy." Even those who experience momentary highs recognize it's not so simple. Stephen Ross, a professor of English at Victoria University, told Sword, "When I'm really going, I just fly. It's what they call 'flow.' I love it. But I know that I'm going to have to go back later and take a third of the prose out."

James Shapiro of Columbia University is more blunt: "It's mostly pain, let's be honest about it. It's grueling. Torture is too strong a word. But it's hard. It's draining."[3]

To write is to struggle, which is why it's so important to make the struggle worthwhile, to the writer above all.

Writing is a skill, developed through deliberate practice.

Writing is like any other skill; the more you practice, the better you get. If you want to learn to play guitar, you might take lessons from an expert, but mostly it's about locking yourself in your room and practice, practice, practice, until you eventually start to make more and more pleasing noises.

Writing is the same, only worse. Skills like playing the guitar or shooting a basketball involve muscle memory, acts that become largely unconscious for an expert practitioner. There is no muscle memory in writing because the brain isn't a muscle.

Writing well is more like becoming a chess master, except it's harder, because unlike writing the patterns of chess do not have to be rewritten as the task changes. Writing is not a game fixed in place. We also don't expect every school-aged kid to become a chess master by the time they turn eighteen.

We overestimate our own proficiency at writing.

Our own writing always makes sense to us because we know what we're trying to say, and even when our specific choices of expression don't quite say what we mean, our brains fill in the blanks.

For example, the first time I typed that sentence, I wrote that our brains "full" in the blanks. I did not notice this error for six days, even though my eyes had run over the sentence many times in the interim. I knew what I meant to say, so my brain was tricking me into thinking I'd said it. Pick just about anything you've written longer than a paragraph and you'll see a similar error.

Students also make these errors because students are human. Students should learn to correct these errors because writing clearly and correctly is important, but being human isn't a sign of catastrophic defect. We often judge students on writing they have not been given the time to polish against standards against which we would never consider holding ourselves.

We also judge student writing on products in which they have little investment beyond passing external assessment, hardly a route to inspiring greatness, or even goodness.

We overestimate our past proficiency at writing.

Not long ago, for the first time in twenty years, I looked at the thesis I submitted to receive my MFA in creative writing.[4] It was the product of three years of monkish dedication to writing fiction, and my memory is that the person who turned in the thesis was good enough to at least be in the publishing game, sending his work into the world with no worse odds of success than any other Joe or Jane.

Twenty years of hindsight revealed the depths of this delusion and why I hadn't yet been published at the time of my graduation; those stories were not worthy of being published. The work wasn't horrible, and yet the gap between it and what would ultimately pass professional muster is apparent. Seeing those stories was like being confronted with the worst picture of your pubescent years, when you look more like something out of Picasso's cubist period than an actual human person.

At least during puberty, because I knew I was in the grip of something powerful and monstrous, I had sufficient self-awareness to know I should lay low and avoid being captured on film if at all possible. At the time of my MFA thesis, I had been pretty sure I was on the cusp of arrival into the world of published writers.

I was certain the thesis would reflect the butterfly I'd become, but nope—I know now I was still very much cocooned. Once we reach a level of proficiency, it is easy to mentally erase the evidence of our own apprenticeships.

We hold students to wrong/unreasonable standards.

Student writing tends to be judged against a standard of "correctness" and resemblance to a kind of "standard" academic writing that doesn't actually exist in nature, the making of which bears little resemblance to the process writers employ when confronted with genuine writing tasks.

When students make mistakes, such as a run-on sentence or a sentence fragment or using the wrong their/there/they're, we judge their writing as defective. But in the wider world, we rarely, if ever, engage with writing by first judging its "correctness." As practicing writers are writing, they never worry about "correctness" until the ideas they are exploring come into focus. People like me are allowed to operate under a different set of values, values that ultimately lead to more effective writing.

In her study of successful writing academics, Helen Sword identified some of the characteristics for writing that writers keep in mind as they work, things like "concision," "structure," "voice," "identity," "clarity," "vocabulary," "agency," "audience," and "telling a story."[5]

When these expert writers think about the sentences themselves they consider not grammar—a word we associate with correctness—but "syntax," the arrangement of words in the expression of an idea.

"Correctness" comes later, and if you're really lucky, much of that work is farmed out to professionals with considerable expertise in that area.

Maybe I've now caused some confusion. I've promised to write a book on why students can't write and what we should do about it, and here I am debunking the idea that students can't write.

Skill-wise and ability-wise, students today are about like students of any other era. In fact, studies show that the "error rate" in student writing has been largely consistent over time, and students today make no more errors than those in 1917, when smartphones were surely not a distraction and texting and Snapchat hadn't allegedly rotted anyone's brain.[6]

Errors have changed—spelling is less of a problem for obvious reasons, while "wrong word" errors (homonyms such as there/their/they're) have increased—but students aren't making more errors than ever. In fact, based on the research of Stanford professor Andrea Lunsford, in which she and her team examined thousands of student artifacts, contrary to the perception of this generation as a texting/emojiing group of illiterates, students today are writing *more* than previous generations.[7]

I am not concerned about students' basic writing skills. Put students in the right situations and they will write clearly, persuasively, even beautifully. But what students are asked to do in school rarely showcases them at their best.

We are in the midst of a shift in literacy. In the words of Lunsford, a pioneer in studies of expository writing, "We're at a crux right now of where we have to figure out as teachers what part of the old literacy is worth preserving. We're trying to figure out how to preserve sustained, logical, carefully articulated arguments while engaging with the most exciting and promising new literacies."[8]

Our collective response to dealing with the changing world of communication in the context of school has created a disconnect where students freely and effectively communicate in other mediums, often using the skills we claim to desire and develop in academic writing. When students turn to school-related tasks, though, those skills seem to disappear.

I am not worried about students' skills, but I am worried about the attitudes and beliefs students bring to writing tasks. Today's average student is often proficient at imitations of writing that pass muster for school, but they struggle mightily with writing tasks that ask them to synthesize and create knowledge. Part of this is because synthesizing and creating knowledge is hard, one of those skills that takes a lot of practice.

But the bigger problem is that they aren't practicing those skills in school. We have students who are highly literate in many ways, but we do not allow them to translate that literacy into the kind of writing that reflects the underlying values of humanistic study.

To build an approach that bridges this divide, we must get back to the core purpose of writing by examining what writing is and how we want students to view writing as they develop their abilities. We have to question what we ask students to do in school and why we ask them to do it. Much of what we claim to be important for the development of students' intellects and abilities does not pass muster; that is, it does not make sense juxtaposed against how writing works and the demands of real-world communication.

Writing is a process that allows us to think and respond to the world at large. It must be open and exploratory, an act where we determine what we mean to say by attempting to say it. Increasingly, writing is a public and even collaborative act, but school often keeps ideas walled off from the world, shared only between student and teacher, and sometimes only shared between student and an anonymous grader.

It's almost worse than having students practicing the training wheels version of writing. It's more like we haven't even let them on a bike.

So, if we want to do better at helping students learn to write, it's worth asking: What are we *doing* when we're writing?

❦ The Writer's Practice

....

As I type these words, I am engaging in the writer's practice.

I have been writing seriously (for over twenty-five years) and teaching writing long enough (twenty years) that the combination of these elements happens subconsciously. My practice is well developed, though we should not confuse "well developed" with faultless or, at times, even functional.

In fact, what you're reading obscures many realities of a writer's practice. By the time a book-buying (or -borrowing) audience sees these words I will have revised, edited, and polished them several times.[1] Trusted readers will have offered feedback. An editor at the publisher will weigh in with his own thoughts. A copyeditor will help polish everything to the highest possible shine. In fact, what I am typing in my initial drafts and what you read in the final version may be quite different in the wording and presentation, even as the idea I'm trying to express remains constant.

Other times as I write, the idea will shift based on the thinking I am doing during the writing itself. What I thought I wanted to say will be altered by the saying. Part of the writer's practice is to be sensitive to this possibility and be open to surprise or revision.

A writer's practice involves discovery, previously hidden things revealed by the doing. Some part or parts of what I am about to articulate about the specific characteristics of the writer's practice will be unknown to me as I first type these words introducing them. They will only reveal themselves to me as I write. This is not something mystical; it is merely a semi-organized, semi-systematic way of thinking.

I wonder what I have to say about the writer's practice.[2]

Practicing Practice

We often think of a doctor or a lawyer having a "practice," but I believe the term applies not just to professions, but to just about any "job."

I spent one summer working as a mail handler in my hometown post office, and you'd better believe there's a right way to go about even what seems on the surface to be purely manual labor. The full-time employees completed the same work I did in a fraction of the time, not just because they were stronger or faster, but because they understood how to work efficiently within our mail delivery system. Their practice of the work, honed through experience, was simply superior. After three months on the job I was much improved and still slower than the regular employees by a significant margin. They had spent more time practicing their practice.

How does a doctor go about doctoring, a lawyer go about lawyering, a mail handler go about mail handling? What does it mean to have a "practice?"

A pediatrician walks into an exam room and is confronted with a child and a parent. The child "doesn't feel good." The parent is worried. The pediatrician conducts an exam, testing pulse and blood pressure, listening to heart and lungs, checking eyes, ears, nose, and throat. Ideally, the exam is systematic and thorough, repeated for each patient, regardless of the child's symptoms.

As the exam is being conducted, the pediatrician is also talking to the parent, asking questions about the child's appetite, for example, or any changes in behavior. The pediatrician notes both a slight fever and a red throat and orders a culture for streptococcus. The pediatrician reassures the parent that right now strep is the chief suspect and that if the test is positive antibiotics should do the trick. If the test isn't positive, they may need to do more testing, or they may want to just wait and see if it's simply a bad flu that will resolve with time, fluids, and rest.

Utterly routine, but what's going on underneath the routine? A practice consists of four primary dimensions:

1. Knowledge (What do doctors know?)
2. Skills (What can doctors do?)
3. Habits of mind (How do doctors think?)
4. Attitudes (What do doctors believe and value about being a doctor?)

We can see all of those things at work in our pediatrician scenario.

One of the reasons medical school is long and grueling is because doctors must "know" a lot. They know anatomy. They know how the digestive, respiratory, endocrine, circulatory, immune, musculoskeletal, and integumentary systems work. They know what *integumentary* means.[3] They know disease processes. They know the appropriate treatments for particular diseases. They know many things I don't even know they know because I'm not a doctor and most of what I know about medicine is gleaned from watching *ER* and *House*.

Importantly, doctors also must know what they don't know and be competent at seeking out additional expertise when they know their own knowledge falls short.

They also have to know other nontechnical things. A pediatrician will need to know how to reassure worried parents. An oncologist will need to know how to deliver the worst news possible to a patient or their loved ones. In today's American medical system, all doctors likely need to know how to digitally chart and account for their work in order to satisfy various bureaucracies.

A doctor's skills may vary depending on specialty, but in the case of a pediatrician, for example, they must know how to do a proper exam of a child. They also must know how to ask appropriate questions of a parent. Part of the practice of a pediatrician's skills is to do all of these "routine" things even if they walk into a room suspecting a particular malady. That means one of the pediatrician's chief skills is possessing the discipline to follow processes and procedures proven effective at diagnosing and treating disease.

While the diagnosis of strep throat in this case may seem simple, it provides an example of how doctors think. As pediatricians take in information, they are sorting through what is and is not important and arranging information in a way that leads to a conclusion—what physicians call a "differential diagnosis."

For experienced doctors, the process of reaching such a diagnosis may be automatic, but a very sophisticated cognitive and critical-thinking process is churning away underneath the surface. This is especially important when the diagnosis is not so obvious, or when a seemingly obvious malady may actually be masking something more serious. Flu (merely temporary and inconvenient) could instead be viral meningitis (sometimes fatal). The intuition we sometimes credit to expert professionals is not mystical but instead a manifestation of years of observation and practice, a skill in and of itself.

When you probe the attitudes and values of doctors you will often find an expressed desire to help people, something enshrined in their professional Hippocratic Oath: First, do no harm. A doctor must also be curious, dedicated to being a "lifelong learner" in order to keep up with advances in medicine that will influence the ways they practice.

Of course, considering the work of a doctor, we see how these categories intertwine in ways that make them inextricable from each other. A surgeon who has knowledge of a particular procedure is not much use if they don't also possess the technical skill to execute that procedure. Anyone can read about delicate brain surgery. Many fewer of us have the dexterity to be brain surgeons.

An oncologist may possess the knowledge of how to best deliver bad news to a patient, but this is also a skill that improves with practice and experience. And here too we see the importance of values and attitudes, as it becomes the doctor's job to attend to the emotional well-being of their patient through the expression of empathy and compassion.

To become expert, doctors must practice their practice. Part of the reason internship and residency periods are required after earning the MD degree is to allow doctors a chance to practice while being supervised by experts. At any given moment, a doctor is engaging in all aspects of their practice, though over time this act of running through a mental checklist becomes unconscious as they learn to think, behave, and act as doctors do.

Or consider a profession I believe is closer to writing than being a doctor: chef.

Chefs must have skills in the form of cooking technique, but they must also possess a deep knowledge of flavors and ingredients, the way salt, fat, and acid combine for effect, and how different techniques affect those traits in different ingredients.

Chefs must be able to think both inductively and deductively. They must be able to look at a list of random ingredients and know how to turn them into delicious food. At the same time, they must be able to taste a finished product and determine what was combined to produce that result.

If you ask any professional chef about their food, they will, in essence, be telling you about what they value. They may mention a tradition like French or Mexican cooking, or attitudes like "clean" or "complex." And of course, flavors—spicy, sweet, savory—can be viewed as expressions of the chef's values as can something like the restaurant's decor or style of service.

A chef's practice, like a doctor's practice, is learned through doing, as they come to understand how knowledge, skills, and techniques intersect. The process of developing those parts of the practice in turn informs their values, what they believe matters when it comes to putting food on the plate.

This becomes a self-reinforcing process. As long as the values are being followed, the skills and knowledge may be used more effectively, creating more ingrained habits of mind, and in turn reinforcing those values, and so on, and so on.

A Writer's Practice

So what is a writer's practice?

How should we think about the attitudes, skills, habits of mind, and knowledge involved in writing?

Attitudes: What Does a Writer Believe and Value about the Act of Writing?

Where to start?

The first attitude all writers must embrace is, in the words of Jeff O'Neal, one-time writing teacher and now CEO of on-line publication group Riot New Media, "You are going to spend your whole life learning how to write, and then you are going to die."

A significant part of the writer's practice—maybe the only part that matters when it comes to attitudes—is recognizing that writing is difficult, that it takes many drafts to realize a finished product, and that you're never going to be as good as you wish.

The gap between one's intentions and the results can never be closed. In my head is the greatest novel in the history of humankind, but something happens between what's in my head and what winds up on the page to diminish the effect.

If I could manage to express my vision with the clarity and conviction it holds inside my head, the concepts in this book would transform the way we talk about and teach writing, lightning bolts of truth jolting my audience to understanding. Because of these inevitable gaps, though, writing is a struggle. This is true for every writer regardless of experience and regardless of past success. There is no such thing as terminal proficiency.

Writers continually build expertise without ever becoming expert. It is like being inside an endlessly right-scrolling game of *Super Mario World*—except you never get to defeat the big boss.

Skills: What Can a Writer Do?

A writer knows how to employ the writing process to conceive, draft, revise, and edit a piece of writing.

As part of the writing process a writer knows how to analyze a rhetorical situation in order to target the message to achieve a specific purpose when communicating to a specific audience. This is the equivalent of chefs who can taste a dish and understand its components so they can remake the dish themselves.

A writer knows how to do research appropriate to the rhetorical situation. For example, if I needed to know the chief export of Bolivia, I need the ability to locate and assess the validity of a source before declaring the answer to be "natural gas."

A writer must be able to think "critically," assessing not only the impact of their own message, but the messages of others they may incorporate into their own writing.

A writer must be able to craft sentences reflecting the meaning they intend as well as demonstrating attention to all aspects of the rhetorical situation.

In this day and age, a writer must be able to use word processing software through typing, dictation, or other adaptive means.

A writer doesn't really need to know how to spell anymore. We have technology handling most of that for us. You just gotta come close while not falling prey to the perils of autocorrect.

Habits of Mind: How Do Writers Think and What Do They Value?

A collaboration of writing teachers drawn from multiple national groups—essentially the Justice League or Avengers of writing instruction—developed a list of eight habits of mind essential for "success in college writing":

- Curiosity: the desire to know more about the world
- Openness: the willingness to consider new ways of being and thinking in the world
- Engagement: a sense of investment and involvement in learning
- Creativity: the ability to use novel approaches for generating, investigating, and representing ideas
- Persistence: the ability to sustain interest in and attention to short- and long-term projects
- Responsibility: the ability to take ownership of one's actions and understand the consequences of those actions for oneself and others
- Flexibility: the ability to adapt to situations, expectations, or demands
- Metacognition: the ability to reflect on one's own thinking as well as on the individual and cultural processes used to structure knowledge[4]

The only change I would make is to change "college writing" to simply "writing." While these habits may take different forms in earlier grades, they should not be reserved for college students alone.

And I may add some things.

Writers must be able to practice empathy in order to write in ways that engage and influence their audience.

Writers must wish to be accurate and truthful.

Writers must be obsessive, which I think of as an order higher than persistent, but perhaps I'm splitting hairs.

Writers should be comfortable with ambiguity and complexity. Even as we seek to provide definitive answers, writers must acknowledge the limits of all ideas.

You're already noticing that, like other professional practices, these different dimensions overlap. The important habits of mind for writing are expressed through those skills and are often inextricably intertwined with attitudes.

As we write, we are likely not consciously aware of our habits of mind, but if they are missing, their absence is apparent in the end results.

Knowledge: What Does a Writer Know?

Writing knowledge has two components:

- Knowledge of writing
- Knowledge of the subject being written about

Writing knowledge is essentially an understanding of all dimensions of the writing practice.

Writing knowledge is built through a combination of study, experience, and reflection. Much of what I've come to know and believe about writing comes from my experiences writing and teaching writing. I've been thinking about these issues for so long that in many cases I've forgotten how I even came to know the things I know.

To build writing knowledge, students must act as writers do. They must engage with all dimensions of the writer's practice. As we'll see, very little of the writing that students are asked to do in school allows for this engagement.

Subject knowledge is complicated when it comes to helping students write better. In reality, young people know lots of things, but they often know little about the things they're asked to write about in school.

Certainly it's important for students to learn new information, because the only way to build knowledge is through exposure to the unfamiliar. But for the unfamiliar to take root and become familiar we need a foundation to build upon. As the writer's practice evolves, as their subject knowledge increases, the frame of reference by which they can evaluate new information expands. Early on, that frame may be quite small, and when we require students to write too far outside that frame, their writing skills may appear wanting, when in reality the students are struggling because they don't have anything to say.

The writing-related tasks we frequently visit upon students would prove difficult for even highly experienced writers. Writing on subjects with which we're newly familiar, in forms that are foreign, and addressed to audiences that are either undefined or unknown (other than "for the teacher") bears little resemblance to the way we write for the world.

Because of this disconnect, we settle for imitations, where students do writing-like or writing-adjacent activities. We expect they will become writers through a process of osmosis that has as much validity as wearing a book on top of your head and expecting the information to seep into your brain.

The Five-Paragraph Essay

The five-paragraph essay is more avatar than direct cause of what ails us. Simply banning its use would have little effect by itself. The ubiquity of the five-paragraph essay is primarily a sign of bad incentives and dysfunctional processes.

The barriers standing in the way to better student writing are systemic. They are baked into the culture of how we approach schooling in the United States. Most of our problems are rooted in a combination of neglect for the big-picture conditions that put students in a position to succeed, and well-meaning quests for solutions that nonetheless fail to address those core problems.

It is as though we are in a leaky boat and 100 percent of our attention has been focused on bailing faster, rather than trying to plug the hole that is letting all the water in. For so long we've been focused on helping students "achieve" that we've lost sight of what this achievement might mean. In teaching writing, this has left our practices largely divorced from the kinds of experiences that help students develop their writing practices.

By itself, the five-paragraph essay isn't necessarily a problem. The form or template appears neutral, an empty vessel into which content can be poured. The five-paragraph essay originally rose out of notions of "correctness," as opposed to classical rhetorical purpose or rhetorical forms, and it has been linked to the Harvard entrance examinations of the late nineteenth century. Even at its inception, the five-paragraph essay was a tool of convenience and standardization.[1]

But there is a difference between an essay with five paragraphs and the "five-paragraph essay."

If writing is like exercise, the five-paragraph essay is like one of those ab belt doohickeys that claim to electroshock your core into a six-pack, so you can avoid doing all those annoying sit-ups.

The five-paragraph essay is an artificial construct, a way to contain and control variables and keep students from wandering too far off track. All they need are the ideas to fill in the blanks. It is very rare to see a five-paragraph essay in the wild; one finds them only in the captivity of the classroom.

This is because writers working with real audiences and real stakes understand that form and content are inseparable. As Kim Zarins, an associate professor at Sacramento State University, says, we need to encourage "students to give their essays the right shape for the thought that each student has."[2]

In reality, every piece of writing is a custom job, not a modular home, and by steering students toward the five-paragraph essay we are denying them the chance to practice real writing by confronting the choices writers must navigate. The five-paragraph essay as employed does not allow students to struggle with the important skills underlying effective writing the same way training wheels don't allow nascent bike riders to practice balance.

The five-paragraph essay has taken root for explicable reasons, even if they are not good ones. They are easy to teach for the purposes of passing standardized assessments. The standardization makes them easier to assign and grade for teachers who are burdened with too many students. If the alternative is no writing at all, surely the five-paragraph essay is better.

And perhaps it is. Many of the form's proponents claim that once students master these basics they can then "play around with them," but we have little evidence that this happens. It certainly isn't in evidence in the first-year college students I work with.

The five-paragraph essay is a shortcut, a compromise enacted so we can efficiently compare students to each other as we drive them toward proficiency or competency.

But proficiency and competency is too low a bar, and efficiency as a value is inconsistent with learning. To make progress we have to pursue excellence and recognize that with learning, the journey is the destination itself, and sometimes that journey may not follow the shortest route.

In the process of writing this book, I've realized that most of what I "know" about teaching writing has come about through my own experimentation and exploration. I now recognize what a gift it has been to be allowed to learn in this way. Essentially, I examine what's happening in a class, identify a particular problem or shortcoming, consider the evidence, and formulate a response. Once I've developed that response, I investigate the scholarship of others and find out that 95 percent of the time someone else has already articulated something similar.

The same pattern has repeated over and over, both in my teaching and my writing: for the learning to be meaningful I must "discover" something for myself that many other people already "know."

This is my practice.

This is identical to the process through which students will become confident and skillful writers. Their identities must transcend being just students in search of grades. During the process of self-invention, students will come to know and understand the world and their place within it.

I can declare some general truism about what makes a good piece of writing, but until students discover this truism on their own, often by doing the opposite and seeing the negative result, it tends to have little currency or impact. Over time, this approach has evolved into a personal pedagogy involving much less direct instruction and many more (sometimes loosely) structured situations to help students "experience" writing, reflect on what's happened, and use what's been learned from that reflection next time around.

This pedagogy has the benefit of being true to how writing works in the world beyond school, but the structure and demands of school often make it hard to resist the lure of aiming for proficiency and smoothing the path toward that goal. Our incentives align against teaching students to write (and think), and instead favor a performance of proficiency.

Prohibitions may prevent disaster, but they also may close off the possibility of great discovery.

If we take away the five-paragraph essay and all the baggage it carries, we'll have to make something new, something that reflects the true challenges of writing.

But before we even get to the specifics of how we can help students explore their writing practices, we must first confront some of the systemic problems that stand in our way.

PART TWO

The Other Necessities

CHAPTER TWO

The Problem of Atmosphere
School Sucks

....

A's above Everything

I like to run an experiment in the second class period of my first-year writing course. It's a required course, and most of the students are conscripts rather than volunteers. Even the students who are English-curious are not looking forward to something billed as "freshman composition" or "academic writing."

I give them a hypothetical: Everyone gets A's in exchange for never doing anything. No classes, no assignments, no reading, no feedback, nothing. We will part ways at the end of this class period, never to see each other again. They just have to make sure they keep their mouths shut because if anyone finds out about our bargain, we'd all get in a lot of trouble.

In a given semester, 80 to 85 percent of my students say they would take this deal.[1]

Their reasons? An A is an A, and A's are good because they help keep the all-important GPA up. Having one less class to worry about would also mean they'd have extra time to dedicate to their other coursework. They could add another course and bump up to 18 or 21 hours of class, which may speed the way to graduation. They could pick up an additional shift at work. They could sleep in. (Lack of sleep is a perpetual complaint for students.)

And English class is, you know, no offense, kind of boring. *What's the trick?* they want to know.

No trick, other than they won't learn anything. Students get this, but I cannot talk them out of their decision. On the first day of class, I tried my best to sell the students on all the vital experiences in the class, but by the second day, no deal. They'll take the A, thank you very much. When I drop the guarantee to a B, I lose about half the students. For 30 to 40 percent, the pain of the course will be worth it if they can get an A, but anything less than that, not so much.

Here is where at one time I would have been tempted to lament the special snowflake, everyone-gets-a-trophy generation who only cares about A's. But it's more complicated than that. I've come to believe something different. Students are not coddled or entitled.

They are defeated.

A Curiosity Crisis

We're supposed to believe that education is empowering, a journey during which students develop their emotional and intellectual abilities. But research shows that school has the opposite effect. From the student perspective, school is a grind, with each year a little less stimulating than the last.

According to an annual survey of over eight hundred thousand students by the Gallup organization, student engagement in school drops every year from the fifth through the eleventh grade.[2]

In 2016, for the first time, a majority of fifth through twelfth graders reported being either "not engaged" (29 percent) or "actively disengaged" (22 percent). Over one-fifth of all students fifth grade or older have effectively checked out of school almost entirely.

This attitude is particularly evident in high school, where on a five-point scale (five meaning "strongly agree" and one meaning "strongly disagree") eleventh graders average 3.66 when asked to respond to the statement, "In the last seven days, I have learned something interesting at school." Fifth graders average 4.30 for the same question.

Each year of school also drains some measure of "hope" out of students. Fifth graders score a 4.62 on "I know I will find a good job in the future." That number drops to 4.20 by eleventh grade. Schooling supposedly focused on making students "college- and career-ready" instead makes students feel less certain of achieving this goal.

Grade to grade we see declines in the percentages of students who "feel safe" in school, who "have fun" in school, and who believe "the adults at my school care about me."

The picture that emerges is bleak: the longer students are exposed to school, the more likely they are to see school and class as a gauntlet to be run, a contest wearing them down a little more each year.

It's no wonder that so many students are openly saying, "School sucks."

"School Sucks"

Bella Bruyere loves "a lot of things; programming, dancing, singing, drawing, learning, teaching, sports, reading, and writing about all of the above."

Unfortunately, she's also decided that "school sucks," but "not because it's boring." She expressed these thoughts in an essay published on *Medium* titled, "Why School Sucks (Hint: It's Not Because It's 'Boring')."[3]

"Read the title," she says. "Now notice that I said school, NOT education. Yes, there is a difference."

Bella contrasts school with her childhood of "reading every day, going on zoo adventures to learn about animals, hiking up to the observatory to stargaze, visiting every museum possible. A seed of curiosity was planted in my mind at an early age and continues to grow today. There is something about having a question and finding the answer that satisfies me, but what really excites me to the core is being able to *do something* with that answer."

Bella's attitude is enough to make any teacher's heart sing. Here is a student who is eager to learn, but her "love" for school changed. Why? "Simple: School stopped being about learning," she says.

She writes that tests and grades and cramming became central to school—and then "an hour in a room of no talking, just bubbling in multiple choice answers while bubbles of anxiety grew in your stomach. School slowly became a place of memorizing facts just long enough to get the A, doing the bare minimum to get into the best college."

Here is a curious, passionate young woman not yet old enough to drive who doesn't see school as a particularly useful place for learning or engaging her curiosities. As the Gallup research shows, she is not an aberration.

Unfortunately, this disconnect between a desire to learn and what happens in school carries over and continues into college.

"I Love Learning; I Hate School"

Susan Blum, a tenured full professor of anthropology at Notre Dame and self-professed lover of all things school, was having a hard time understanding why so many of the students at her elite institution didn't feel the same.

In 2002, following a semester in which a required first-year course on "childhood" did not go well, the students from which she'd been "expecting impressive things" instead appeared disengaged and uninterested, and one student evaluation read, "I don't think professor Blum likes college students."[4]

She writes, "I was discouraged, wounded, disappointed. I grumbled to my colleagues that my students put almost no care into their work. They refused the intellectual bounty we offered them." She observed that her students were "smug about their accomplishments without making the effort to excel." They expected credit for simply attending. One student—"the most memorable"—said in a reflective essay "that because of his admission to this illustrious university his family had achieved greatness."

Professor Blum had always loved school and thrived in its atmosphere; she could not understand how her students—by all possible accounts accomplished, prepared, among the educational elite—could arrive at a place like Notre Dame with such negative attitudes toward school.

So she made use of the tools of anthropology and started studying students, talking to them, soliciting their attitudes and experiences of school. The research resulted in her book, "*I Love Learning; I Hate School*," the title drawn from the testimony of a "high achieving college student" who nonetheless hated school the same way Isabella Bruyere hates school.

In Professor Blum's book I recognized traits of the students in my first-year writing class who valued an A over everything, for whom learning was an airy abstraction, while grades—even those entirely unconnected to achievement—were something meaningful. Students had become cynical about school. School counts, but it doesn't *matter*.

It is tempting to lay blame with the students, to consider their attitude a defect of character or an absence of gumption, but Susan Blum and I see it differently. In Professor Blum's words, "This now universal system of institutionalized schooling not only destroys joy and curiosity, and creates dropouts and failures, winners and losers. It also often fails to achieve even the goals we set, however assessed and however defined."[5]

Given the systems we've created, what incentives do students have to value "learning" over grades? None that I can see.

School does not appear to provide an atmosphere conducive to learning. It certainly doesn't value curiosity or exploration. As we'll see later, this is especially damaging when it comes to learning to write.

But there is a more important and immediate consequence. School is making students ill.

School Is Bad for You

If you spend much time teaching, you will inevitably experience what I call the student "face crumble," the moment when some bit of news causes a student's features to collapse into a mask of distress and vulnerability and helplessness. Some students will start crying, but most don't. The face crumble is usually over in a flash, an unguarded moment as the mask slips. For years, the face crumble was almost exclusively reserved for news of a failing grade or something like a plagiarism accusation.

But four or five years ago, I began to witness an unprecedented number of face crumbles. Whereas they had previously been confined to individual conferences, face crumbles now were happening in class, often in response to what I had considered otherwise innocuous information.

I will never forget the student whose face crumbled when I started a period with an enthusiastic/excited, "Only two weeks left of class!" This student did start to cry a little and then smiled through the embarrassment. "I don't know why I did that," they said.[6]

I had my suspicions, suspicions later confirmed when the student came by my office and I gently prodded as to what was going on. The student had another short cry. "I just can't imagine finishing everything I have to do," they said.

This student of mine is not alone. Every year the Cooperative Institutional Research Program (CIRP) at the Higher Education Research Institute (HERI) at UCLA conducts the *American Freshman National Norms* survey, exploring a range of experiences and attitudes among the over one hundred thousand respondents. The research shows a student body whose physical and mental well-being degrades with each successive matriculating year.

In 1985, only 18.3 percent of college-bound students said they "frequently" felt "overwhelmed by all I had to do" during senior year of high school.

In 2011, that number had increased to 28.5 percent.

In 2016 we were up to just shy of 41 percent.[7]

Unsurprisingly, the incidence of depression in teenagers has increased by more than 35 percent between 2005 and 2015. During this time, the demand for campus mental health services has been "soaring," with many schools overwhelmed beyond capacity.[8]

The American College Health Association found that the percentage of students reporting "overwhelming anxiety" within a twelve-month period increased from an already-high 50 percent in 2011 to 62 percent in 2016.[9]

These alarming statistics do not mean that students are somehow defective or mentally weaker than previous generations. In reality, we have created an atmosphere that is toxic to student mental health.

I have seen this in working with students, not just the face crumbles, but college freshmen who report having had their first school-related anxiety attacks in grade school. Many students hope college will be a fresh start after the grind of high school, but the legacy of stress and anxiety is difficult to escape. For so long, school has been about performance divorced from learning, so it's difficult to find value in anything other than an A.

This fear of "failure," of anything less than an "A," is pervasive. It is the leading cause of face crumbles. These are not students who are afraid to work hard or who lack grit. It is hard to fathom the kind of grit it takes to drag oneself to class in the midst of an anxiety attack, something I have seen students do more than once.

I tell students that writing is an "extended exercise in failure," but it is a noble failure, a failure born of lofty, self-generated goals, where we reach for the stars and land on the moon. We fall short only because we believe we're capable of more. This brand of failure makes us hungry to get back in the arena to make use of what we've learned the last time around.

Unfortunately, students arrive at college looking at school as a different kind of arena, entering the classroom in a defensive crouch, having survived an academic version of the *The Hunger Games*. I could rewrite this chapter on a weekly basis, adding additional illustrations of the damage being done to students. I could mention the "suicide clusters" in Santa Clara County, California, and Fairfax, Virginia, where pressure to perform academically was identified by the Centers for Disease Control as a contributing factor.[10]

I could share the suicide note of a 16-year-old from a southern California high school who loved his family, his friends, and his coaches, but who could not withstand the pressure of his "highly competitive" high school: "One slipup makes a kid feel like the smallest person in the world. You are looked at as a loser if you don't go to college or if you get a certain GPA or test score. All anyone talks about is how great they are or how great their kid is. It's all about how great I am. It's never about the other kid. The kid who maybe does not play a sport, have a 4.0 GPA, but displays great character." He said his public high school felt like a private school. "So much pressure is placed on the students to do well that I couldn't do it anymore."[11]

It is hard to imagine a less conducive atmosphere in which to learn anything, let alone practice writing, an activity that requires time, space, and freedom to fail.

It gets worse. Not only are students subject to internal pressures created by school atmospheres that place a greater value on "achievement" than learning; we're also forcing them to do this work while being under near constant surveillance.

The Problem of Surveillance

The Wrong Times for Real-Time Data

My closest encounter with real-time data has been in hospital rooms, when a loved one is hooked up to the equipment and we can see and even hear a moment-to-moment readout of pulse, respiration, oxygenation, all the base indicators of life.

It is the oxygenation number that got to me when my father was sick, on his way to dying of cancer.

The pulse oximeter is the thingy that clamps to the patient's finger and measures the oxygen saturation of the blood. If you are walking around and healthy that saturation is 100 percent. If you are in the hospital and ill it may be less than that; in fact, it may vary up and down through the 90s, occasionally dipping into the 80s. When you are spending entire days in your dying father's hospital room and your primary activity has been watching the numbers on the screen and you see this happening—into the 80s, and now the 70s—you begin to freak out a bit.

You look around frantically for a nurse or a doctor, not wanting to be alarmist, but also not wanting to do nothing if something should be done. You know nothing other than the numbers, and 72 is less than 100, a lot less. A part of your brain you do your best to ignore is aware that your father is going to die, but nobody has led you to believe that that day is today, when you are the only one in the room because your mother needs an occasional break from her near-constant vigil.

Do you know who isn't constantly responding to real-time data in hospitals? Medical professionals. The monitors are equipped with alarms for sudden occurrences, and everything is recorded for posterity, but you do not see nurses and doctors obsessing over every last bleep and bloop—because they have something necessary for working with data: judgment.

And so when the nurse comes in and sees the pulse oximeter number is lower than one would wish, rather than calling down a team of additional professionals, she checks the patient's finger and sees that . . . yep . . . the little doohickey has slipped a little.

You realize that if you're going to stay in that room, you need to turn your back to those monitors because they are a form of torture.

On the one hand, collecting that real-time data in this situation is a necessity. A critically ill patient must be monitored. On the other hand, the terrified family may not need to be constantly subjected to that data.

As we collect more and more data about all aspects of our lives, the urge to quantify what might better be simply experienced is incredibly tempting.

We often hear the benefits of having access to "real-time" data in education.

But is that access always beneficial? Who should have it? What kind of data are we talking about? When does real-time data cross the line into surveillance? What happens to students when outside intervention, triggered by "data," becomes an expectation they bring into the learning experience?

Is real-time data compatible with the goals of education?

No. Almost certainly not.

Its temptations have us swinging at too many pitches and valuing the wrong things.

Why Monitor?

I will never forget the moment I ditched my FitBit. I woke up one morning feeling good, energetic and sharp, until I checked the FitBit data on my sleep and saw that I'd had over thirty periods of "restlessness" during the night.

Suddenly I felt exhausted and had to fight the urge to go back to bed. I had felt good, but the FitBit was telling me I should be near-comatose. But why was I crediting this data over my lived experience in the moment?

We could argue that quantified data may reveal important information to which we'd otherwise be blind, information that may be necessary for improvement. "Moneyball" has transformed how baseball teams think about their players, for example.

When it comes to fitness devices, however, improvement seems to be more elusive. Numerous studies have shown that using the devices has little connection to weight loss. In one study covering a two-year period, those with access to the technology lost an average of 7.7 pounds.

Those without access to the technology lost 13 pounds.[1]

Researchers believe the fitness technology has the unfortunate effect of redirecting the attention of the dieter from the most important factor in losing weight: what and how much we eat. Hitting those ten thousand steps a day creates a sense of achievement, which is great, but if the goal is to lose weight, it isn't the kind of achievement we should be focused on.

Because we can count them, steps become a proxy for fitness, but steps are not fitness.[2] When we focus on the thing we can conveniently and accurately count, we may crowd out more important aspects of fitness that are more difficult to count, and in doing so, distort the entire process.

Something similar is happening in education. We want to track "learning," but learning is hard to quantify, since it happens inside of students and occasionally arrives after a period of delay. Any writing instructor will tell you about the email received from a student a semester, or a year, or even five years removed from a course, in which they will report, "*Now* I know what you meant when you talked about . . ."

The data we can capture in education can be misleading. And as we'll see when discussing the problem of standardization, when we let incomplete data drive our curriculum, we cause serious problems.

The Perils of Parent Portals

With advances in technology, we have achieved something close to the collection of real-time data in K–12 classrooms. This data is often shared via "parent portals," digital dashboards designed to transmit information to parents of school-aged children about attendance, grades, assignments, behaviors—you name it. There is now virtually no delay between a student's suboptimal academic or social performance and parental notification.

Apps like ClassDojo are used to track every moment of student behavior and performance, sometimes displaying this information on smartboards broadcast in the classrooms themselves, for example identifying those who are successfully following directions (gold star) or those whose dogs ate their homework (frowny face).[3]

This real-time tracking becomes a narrative of the collective class experience, even as it is happening, as illustrated by Natasha Singer, writing about ClassDojo in the *New York Times*:

> For better or for worse, the third graders in Greg Fletcher's class at Hunter Elementary School always know where they stand.
>
> One morning in mid-October, Mr. Fletcher walked to the front of the classroom where an interactive white board displayed ClassDojo, a behavior-tracking app that lets teachers award points or subtract them based on a student's conduct. On the board was a virtual classroom showing each student's name, a cartoon avatar and the student's scores so far that week.
>
> "I'm going to have to take a point for no math homework," Mr. Fletcher said to a blond boy in a striped shirt and then clicked on the boy's avatar, a googly-eyed green monster, and subtracted a point.

The program emitted a disappointed pong sound, audible to the whole class—and sent a notice to the child's parents if they had signed up for an account on the service.[4]

Imagine a real-time ranking of your school performance. How would you begin to think and feel about school? How would you feel about taking a risk, or exploring an idea about which you're uncertain? What would be your strategy to get through the school day?

It would have killed me. Even the 1970s version of the data board caused me enough distress to remember its impact more than forty years later.

As a preschool child, I had some issues with fine motor coordination. I couldn't use scissors and I couldn't color inside the lines. In prekindergarten testing my performance on these tasks was troubling enough that there was talk of maybe waiting a year before starting school.

And then my mother pulled out a book and asked if it mattered that I could read.

I couldn't color, but I could read. Being raised in a bookstore that my mom had started when I was a year old probably had something to do with it. My fine motor coordination issues continue to this day. My handwriting is a fright. Don't ask me to craft. In a contest of quality, you would hang the average first grader's art on the refrigerator in a place of honor far before anything I could conjure.

Today's "college- and career-ready" kindergarten would probably have suited me well in terms of achievement, but back in the 70s it was coloring and drawing a good deal of the time. My Thanksgiving turkey hand-tracing craft project resulted in a creature that looked like something spawned in a post-Chernobyl radioactive hellscape.

We also had a gold-star board used for marking achievements. I'm sure I did well in learning my alphabet, but I only remember two of the items, zipping your own coat and tying your own shoes. I remember those because I was the last kid in class to get those stars. I remember crying over my shoelaces, trying to practice at home. At recess, even in the frigid Midwest, I'd pretend I wanted my coat open because I'd get hot.

It's possible I was an oversensitive kid, and it's likely my memory has distorted reality. At the time, I might not have outwardly displayed much stress. But that's part of the point. We may not be able to immediately observe surveillance-driven distress. Kids may not even be fully aware of the origins of their own feelings. Children in classrooms that use ClassDojo are being acculturated to a world where they must comply 100 percent of the time or risk censure. What effect is this likely to have on their attitudes toward school and learning?

When I think back to my kindergarten year, I remember most of all the ways I was defective, even as I was reading while my peers were still learning the alphabet.

With the new tracking technology, there are very few parts of a student's day not being measured and cataloged. Education reformers believe if we crunch enough of this data, we will unlock a secret to how to better teach students, but this assumes that learning works the same for everyone, that there is a secret sauce to learning.

But what if learning really is a process that happens inside each individual a little differently? What if students need sufficient freedom in order to find a path that works for them?

Surveillance and Compliance

It gets worse. ClassDojo tends to be used in classrooms for children of privilege who have significant educational advantages. Less advantaged students are subject to surveillance we'd more likely associate with prison than school.

Hero (formerly Hero K12) is ClassDojo extended to every moment of the school day, where scan-card technology and handheld devices are used to track and quantify every interaction into a system of demerits and rewards. Being on time or doing extra credit allow you to cut to the front of the lunch line. Tardiness means you wait with the rest of the rabble or can't attend the pep rally. A formal caste system is dictated by the data collection.

The system allows for no human discretion. We do not know why a student may habitually arrive late—perhaps because a younger sibling needs escorting to school when a parent is unavailable. We do not care that a student nods off in class because they are hungry. What matters is not the individual, but the fact of "lateness" or "inattention," as though this were the most important variable for learning.

Some of the teachers Natasha Singer spoke to express appreciation for how ClassDojo helps them manage class behavior by focusing on positive rewards as doled out through the app. This makes it easier, in the words of one teacher, for students to "stay on task."

In theory this sounds great. We've always allowed windows into the classroom via report cards and parent/teacher conferences. What's the harm in making those windows wider and letting more light in?[5]

As a long-time college instructor, I perceive plenty of harm. In fact, if given the choice, I'd shut down the parent portals entirely.

As we outsource our interactions with students to surveillance technology rooted in systems that value compliance, we short-circuit important parts of the learning process.

The Pleasures and Perils of Freedom

Two of the most important traits for students to develop to succeed at education in general, and writing in particular, are agency and resilience.

Agency is simply the ability to act and think under one's own initiative.

Resilience is the ability to get up when you've fallen down, to learn from your own failures.

Consider a child who takes a bad spill when the child thinks no one is looking. I'm not talking an oopsie, but an actual knee-scraper, a legit owie. Let's say the kid is charging after something—say, a ball or a dog. Maybe the thing is entirely imaginary. We've all known kids like that.

The moment before the spill was a good one, an exciting one, and then suddenly . . . ouch.

They feel pain because it hurts. They roll over, inspect the abrasion. They have seen this before. It is red and throbby. It is the kind of thing dad or mom would fuss over if they saw it, a walk inside for some of that gooey ointment, a kiss to make it all better. There would be tears, a relief because the tears bring attention and attention is love.

But this time, there is no one around and it hurts, but it has hurt before and eventually it stopped hurting, sometimes even before dad or mom kissed it better.

Maybe mom and dad aren't always necessary, not when there is something to be chased after.

Brush the bits of dirt or gravel away, ouch again. A tear, a prelude to more? Still, no mom or dad or anyone.

That thing that seemed so interesting is getting away. Back of hand across cheek, tears wiped away. Better get up and get after it.

What would have happened if the child had never been allowed to self-soothe? What if so many protections were in place that they never had the chance to fall in the first place?

One of the common criticisms of the current generation of college students is that they lack this kind of resilience. However, rather than being rooted in an inherent lack of character, any perceived lack of resilience, I believe, is caused by two factors:

- In academic matters, we track and punish (both implicitly and explicitly) too much, too often, and this tracking and punishing make students sensibly risk averse.

- Because we track too much and intervene from the outside too often, we don't allow students to solve their own problems.

Part of that problem solving must allow students to decide for themselves what "matters." One of the reasons students are so often grade driven is because grades are the only currency of value in school. A school less focused on "achievement" and more focused on learning would naturally allow students to practice agency and resiliency. As we will see, writing is perhaps uniquely positioned as a route to helping students practice both of these behaviors.

Another complicating factor is an overall culture in which "success" is a limited resource, reserved for a fortunate few, and even small slip-ups may derail an entire future. Students believe that a "failure" like a C in a class will result in significant negative consequences, which fuels the anxiety and depression.

In this kind of atmosphere, students don't have sufficient space to screw up and face appropriate but not disastrous consequences.

Having the opportunity to screw up and pay the (appropriate) price is one of the most important parts of becoming a resilient adult, of developing the kind of self-regulating behaviors that will be a big part of future success and happiness.

Real-time data makes it too easy and too tempting to intervene, outsourcing responsibility from the student to the parent, rather than requiring students to remedy problems through their own actions and agency.

Jessica Lahey, both a parent and a teacher, argues in *The Gift of Failure: How the Best Parents Learn to Let Go So Their Children Can Succeed* that an important part of developing resiliency involves taking risks, seeking out challenges that may be beyond our abilities but that serve as a compelling struggle engaged under our own initiative.[6]

For failure to be meaningful, we also must occasionally face consequences and the appropriate anxiety that comes with knowing we're off track, and punishment when our sins are later revealed.

Real-time data makes it too tempting for authority figures to intervene before failure can even occur. The interventions are well-meaning—students are off track when they must be on task!—but the consequence is that students are simultaneously stressed out because they know they're being watched, and too safe, because they know someone is going to catch them before they hit the ground, let alone scrape their knee.

School has never lacked for feedback. We have report cards, phone calls or emails home, parent-teacher conferences. There was a time when these were all better than sufficient.

Has the world changed so much that students need near-constant surveillance in order to stay on track academically? What are the benefits of always being on track and on task, anyway?

Here is where our poor proxies for "learning" create the most troubling distortions in the learning process.

The False God of Attention

To some, merely tracking performance is for laggards. Why not intervene sooner, at the very instant students start to even slightly waver off the prescribed path?

Schooling puts a lot of stock in "attention" as a key to learning. In schools like the KIPP (Knowledge is Power Program) charters or other so-called no-excuses atmospheres, attention is so important that things like sitting up and tracking the speaker are mandatory behaviors, and teachers are instructed to give real-time corrections to students who do things like rest their chins on their hands. While not rooted in technology, the entire ethos of these sorts of schools is still based on surveillance. Students must be "scholars" every moment of every day, and the chief goal of scholars in this world is to pay attention to the teacher.

This is a very narrow definition of scholar, one that is far more rooted in compliance than learning and education. If you ever have to ask someone if they're paying attention, the answer is likely to be "no," but that doesn't necessarily mean they weren't doing something important.

If we're talking about education and learning, attention by itself is something of a false god.

The KIPP verboten chin-on-hand is the iconic pose of Rodin's *The Thinker*, a solitary figure meant to embody deep contemplation. But giving students time and space to think is a dangerous proposition when compliance is so valued. Thinking is both invisible and unknowable, and even ungovernable. We don't know if Rodin's thinker is contemplating the state of the human condition or wondering if the roast lamb he had for lunch tasted a little off. Rather than risk a wayward thought, schools have put a premium on attention to the point many students are even medicated so they may better perform this compliance.

And make no mistake, it is a performance, primarily for the benefit of teachers and those who believe learning happens best in orderly spaces, a contention for which we have no compelling evidence. If your mind is attending to sitting up straight so as not to risk punishment from the teacher, how much of the lesson can you be absorbing?

Welcome to the Panopticon

The next generation of student surveillance technology aims to track not only behaviors and outcomes but "attention."

Well, not attention so much as the performance of attention as tracked by cameras utilizing facial analysis algorithms, as proposed by a program called Nestor, by LCA Learning. Nestor "uses students' webcams to analyze eye movements and facial expressions and determine whether students are paying attention to a video lecture." The developers are hoping to eventually extend the software into the live classroom where the software could send "real-time notifications to students whenever they're not paying attention."[7]

It's not clear if the reminder to pay attention will come via electric shock or some other method. Maybe attention will be graded. If so, get ready for a generation of students who have trained themselves to never blink.

It gets more absurd. In October 2017, BrainCo Inc. received $15 million in funding from Chinese investors to develop their new technology, whereby "students sit at desks wearing electronic headbands that report EEG data back to a teacher's dashboard, and that information purports to measure students' attention levels."

Never mind that no one has any idea if it works. BrainCo's presentation at a 2016 Consumer Electronics Show was voted the "most cringeworthy demonstration,"[8] causing some to question whether BrainCo is selling digital snake oil.

For what it's worth, most neuroscientists are skeptical, but BrainCo still aims to be "the first company to quantify this invisible metric of student engagement."

It's invisible, and yet they think they can detect it. This is a belief in technology that is nearly fantastical.

I'm willing to bet that those Chinese investors will have realized they might as well have flushed their $15 million down the toilet by the time you read this sentence, but the question we should be asking extends beyond whether this technology "works." Even if this technology works exactly as intended, will it help students learn?

The answer is no. Attention and engagement are not synonyms.

What's More Important Than Attention? Lots of Stuff

By valuing attention so highly, we crowd out other behaviors that may be critical to learning. Strategies like those used at KIPP and other "no-excuses" schools are only necessary because school is a rather grim march through proficiencies, rather than a place in which to engage with curiosities. The downside is that students who are steeped in these no-excuses experiences, despite sometimes stellar academic records, are ill prepared for the different challenges of higher education and the independent working world.

Darryl Robinson, a graduate of a no-excuses charter school in Washington, DC, described his first year at Georgetown as a full scholarship student, a year when he "quickly felt unprepared and outmatched" and had to play "catch-up."

In high school Robinson "maintained good grades simply by listening to my teachers and giving them what they wanted to hear: themselves. I could go to class, pay attention, and as long as I was respectful, I stood out as a great student."

After getting a D- on his first writing assignment in his college English class, an assignment he thought he'd done well on, Robinson recognized the difference between his and his peers' experiences: "I did what I'd been taught growing up in school: memorize and regurgitate information. Other Georgetown freshmen from better schools had been trained to form original, concise thoughts within a breath, to focus less on remembering every piece of information, word for word, and more on forming independent ideas. I was not. I could memorize and recite facts and figures, but I didn't know how to think for myself."[9]

Darryl Robinson has been conditioned to become what sociologist Joanne Golann calls a "worker-learner." Golann says, "The meticulous practices adopted by [no-excuses schools] to ensure academic achievement have the paradoxical effect of producing worker-learners—students who monitor themselves, hold back their opinions, and defer to authority—rather than lifelong learners."[10]

Once in college, where students are expected to be "interactional learners," the Darryl Robinsons of the world struggle. What should be the byproducts of an education—learning and personal growth—have been sacrificed for order and (very limited) "achievement."

The kid staring out the window daydreaming may be heading for failure—or may be conjuring the next iPhone. It is hard to know and impossible to measure, and that impossibility makes us deeply uncomfortable. But research shows that daydreaming may be a key to learning, a way for our brains to sort and process what we've been experiencing.

Mental breaks both enhance creativity and facilitate problem solving.[11] Just about everyone has experienced the sensation of butting your head against the wall of an intractable problem, taking a break or sleeping on it, and coming back to find the solution suddenly seeming obvious.

This isn't to say that class should be chaos or we should suddenly grant wool-gathering priority over focused work in the classroom, but thinking and learning require time, space, and freedom. Relentlessly tracking students in real time to help them "achieve" does little to foster an atmosphere conducive to learning and discovery.

In fact, given what we know about how student disengagement increases with each year of schooling, and the increasing incidence of anxiety and depression, it is more likely that the way we monitor students and insist on compliance is doing more harm than good.

There is no greater tool for enforcing compliance than the standardized test.

The Problem of Assessment and Standardization

In 1983, the National Commission on Excellence in Education, established by Terrell Bell, President Ronald Reagan's Secretary of Education, launched the last thirty-five years of school reform with a dire warning, a report titled *A Nation at Risk*: "Our Nation is at risk. Our once unchallenged preeminence in commerce, industry, science, and technological innovation is being overtaken by competitors throughout the world. . . . the educational foundations of our society are presently being eroded by a rising tide of mediocrity that threatens our very future as a Nation and a people. What was unimaginable a generation ago had begun to occur—others are matching and surpassing our educational achievements."[1]

The diagnosis of *A Nation at Risk* is so dire that it's hard to believe the country stayed intact long enough to enact much later attempts at school reform, such as No Child Left Behind (2002), Race to the Top (2009), or the even more recent push to establish a national set of educational standards known as the Common Core.

In fact, the narrative of *A Nation at Risk* in 1983—that we are a nation of "idlers" comfortable with a "rising tide of mediocrity," as demonstrated by substandard student scores on standardized tests—is almost identical to the public rationale for the push to adopt the Common Core State Standards in 2012. David Coleman, the CCSS "architect," was fond of citing ACT scores showing "only one in every four high school graduates is ready to do college-level reading, writing, science, and computation."[2]

Almost thirty years, and the story has barely changed a whit.

That "failing schools / failing students" narrative is similar to the perennial complaints about students' writing abilities. A kernel of truth—students are not at the level we wish them to be—is inflated into a dire crisis, and because we are in a crisis "something must be done," whether or not that something has a meaningful connection to the actual problems.

In reality, *A Nation at Risk* was the equivalent of the Gulf of Tonkin incident in Vietnam, a rationale crafted with some measure of good intention that has created a cycle of endless doubling down on a flawed premise.

The dire warnings of *A Nation at Risk* included these specific concerns:

> These deficiencies come at a time when the demand for highly skilled workers in new fields is accelerating rapidly. For example:
>
> - Computers and computer-controlled equipment are penetrating every aspect of our lives—homes, factories, and offices.
> - One estimate indicates that by the turn of the century millions of jobs will involve laser technology and robotics.
> - Technology is radically transforming a host of other occupations. They include health care, medical science, energy production, food processing, construction, and the building, repair, and maintenance of sophisticated scientific, educational, military, and industrial equipment.

In 1983, when future Facebook founder Mark Zuckerberg was a year away from being born, we were being warned of being ill-prepared for the coming technological revolution. Somehow we survived to successfully enter the Internet age.

The response to *A Nation at Risk* has been a thirty-plus-year regime of assessment and accountability testing that, in the words of Harvard professor of education and former grade school teacher Daniel Koretz, is nothing more than a "charade" in which we "pretend" to make schools better.

Koretz argues: "Pressure to raise scores on achievement tests dominates American education today. It shapes what is taught and how it is taught. It influences the problems students are given in math class (often questions from earlier tests), the materials they are given to read, the essays and other work they are required to produce, and often, the manner in which teachers grade this work."[3]

There is little doubt that the reform efforts since *A Nation at Risk* have delivered few meaningful improvements. This is true even by the preferred measurements of education reformers—standardized tests. Recently, even dyed-in-the-wool supporters of testing- and accountability-based school reform have begun to recognize the limitations of standardized tests to give us meaningful feedback about what and how students are learning. In responding to Koretz's *The Testing Charade*, Rick Hess of the strongly pro-reform American Enterprise Institute admitted that "we have done a lot of genuinely stupid stuff in the name of 'accountability,'" including erecting teacher evaluation systems that Hess calls "mindless, dangerous, and destructive."[4]

Robert Pondiscio of the pro-reform Thomas B. Fordham Institute, who for decades has been near the center of education reform, looks at its legacy and laments, "A conceptual failure lies at the heart of ed reform's underperformance: the mistaken assumption that education policy, not classroom practice, is the most important lever to pull to drive enduring improvement." Pondiscio recognizes that top-down initiatives tracked through standardized tests have distorted classroom practices in ways that have disconnected "schooling" from "learning." He says, "We have mostly overplayed our hand, overstated our expertise, and outspent our moral authority by a considerable margin as we morphed from idealism to policymaking. Education reform's policy prerogatives have transformed schooling in ways that parents don't much like—test-based accountability, in particular, focused on just two subjects—and without clear and lasting benefits to justify them."[5]

Hess, Pondiscio, and others who fully embraced the corporate reform practices launched by *A Nation at Risk* are chastened, but somehow they retain some measure of faith that we can test our way to better schools. But how much more do we need to know before we can accept that this approach will not work? We've been trying it for thirty years without meaningful success; surely by this point it's time to change the narrative.

In truth, we didn't need all these years of fruitless pursuit of meaningful and actionable standardized tests to know standardization is a poor fit for assessing writing. We merely needed to consider the complexity of writing, and the limits of tests.

The Testing Charade

The results of a test can tell us lots of things, but some of those things may have nothing to do with what we think we're testing.

For example, researchers from the University of South Carolina found that performance on a standardized math exam was correlated with the arrival of students' families receiving their SNAP (Supplemental Nutrition Assistance Program) benefits.

Being tested around the time of receiving the aid resulted in higher scores. If students were three or more weeks removed from their family's receiving benefits, they scored lower. This held true even when testing the same child.

In other words, those tests were really measuring student hunger.[6]

Most of the standardized tests we give students are susceptible to similar unintended variables. Average scores on the SAT are almost universally correlated with household income: more income, higher scores.[7] Reformers who put their faith in testing believe they are a route to meritocracy. More often, they are x-rays that reveal existing structural inequalities.

Reformers approached the gaps in achievement with noble intent, believing in educational achievement as a potential leveling force in society. But putting their faith in tests and focusing their energies on "raising scores" through curricular and managerial interventions has prevented us from having a deeper and more difficult discussion about the true causes of those gaps: systemic barriers rooted in race and poverty,[8] which initiatives such as No Child Left Behind and Race to the Top only reinforce.

The achievement gap between wealthy and poor students has actually *increased* during this era of school reform.[9] When achievement is framed as a competition and places at the top appear scarce, inevitably those with more resources will do better. There is no rising tide lifting all boats in our approach to education reform over the last thirty years. Some students have access to seaworthy vessels while others are left swimming for their lives.

Campbell's Law

Standardized testing has made us captive to "Campbell's Law," named for Don Campbell, a pioneer in evaluation studies: "The more any quantitative social indicator is used for social decision making, the more subject it will be to corruption pressures, and the more apt it will be to distort and corrupt the social processes it is intended to monitor."

Put another way, if a single metric is deemed to be of value, all other metrics become unimportant. Worse, behaviors will shift in order to affect that metric, no matter if the behaviors reflect the underlying goal or not.

Let's say we observed that couples who kiss each other good-bye in the morning tend to have happier marriages, so we start telling people that the key to a happy marriage is to kiss each other good-bye every morning. While getting a nice peck before parting ways may be a good thing, it does nothing to address the underlying behaviors that make for happy marriages. That morning kiss is only important as a byproduct of those emotionally healthy practices. People kissing each other good-bye is a manifestation of deep-rooted feelings of love and connectedness. When the kiss becomes the goal itself, far more important factors get neglected.

As Daniel Koretz argues in *The Testing Charade,* this focus has steadily led to increasing perversions when it comes to instruction, weeding out supposedly extraneous subjects like art and music, and social activities such as recess, to dedicate more time to test preparation. Koretz even believes that some of the gains we do perceive in the testing may be illusory, the product of focus on test prep strategies, rather than meaningful learning.

In some cases, the better a score on a standardized test, the less students might be learning. Any "miracle" school likely has an alternative explanation. The New Orleans "miracle" following Hurricane Katrina ("the best thing that happened in the education system in New Orleans," according to Education Secretary Arne Duncan), showed that any increase in test scores came from flushing the most disadvantaged students out of the system.[10]

Testing and accountability policies have actively incentivized cheating. The systemic cheating in the Atlanta and Washington, DC, school systems has been well documented.[11] Pressure to perform on the tests or risk losing funding or being terminated rippled through schools and administrations, resulting in these massive scandals.

Even "genuine" gains in test scores may come at the expense of other important aspects of school, as test prep dominates the curriculum. It is also not incidental that the decline in student engagement with school coincides with greater emphasis on standardized tests.

Students see schooling as separate from learning because they're living the compromises that must be made in order to measure up on these assessments.

They understand the difference between work that is meaningful and work that "counts." Because of standardized assessments these concepts are increasingly separate.

This is why students tell us, "I love learning; I hate school." It's why engagement drops with each year of schooling, and it's a big reason why so many students are anxious.

Our goal with testing, Koretz says, should be to "improve the cognitive abilities" of students. If this were our goal, we would be concerned with not only tests of memory or attention—what most standardized tests boil down to—but "executive functions" as well, which include flexibility, lateral thinking, and empathy, abilities that are not only absent from standardized assessments, but are explicitly devalued when standardized assessments dominate curriculum.

Standardized tests tell us little about the process of learning, and often indicate even less about what may or may not be happening in the classroom.

Christopher Tienken, professor of education at Seton Hall, has been able to predict standardized test scores with 75 percent accuracy using only demographic data, such as income, percentage of people in poverty, and percentage of people in the community with bachelor's degrees.

Tienken argues that tests as currently employed do nothing to "diagnose learning." They are at best "monitoring devices." He says, "The bottom line is this: Whether you're trying to measure proficiency or growth, standardized tests aren't the answer."[12]

Even if we're willing to accept a tradeoff of emotional harm in the form of increased stress or diminished enthusiasm for school, there's no evidence that standardized testing regimes help improve student cognition in a meaningful way.

This is especially true when it comes to writing, because the very nature of writing makes it impossible to standardize. Writing assessments that can withstand standardization are fundamentally incompatible with the experiences students must have in order to develop their writing practices.

The more students are subjected to high-stakes standardized testing of their writing, the less they learn.

Testing What We Can, Not What Matters

In the early grades we test "reading" rather than "writing," and the reading tests themselves focus on the useful but relatively narrow skill of "close reading." Reading closely, seeking to understand the impact of different authorial choices and making inferences from the texts to prove comprehension of not just the piece in general, but some of its component parts, is essentially what happens as we read, as long as we're reading carefully. We are often not consciously aware of this underlying process, but as the text works its magic, we respond as readers. With hindsight, we can closely examine the text to understand the reasons for those responses.

So far so good. However, when this aspect of reading is translated into something that fits inside a multiple choice question where only one answer is allowed, the complexity of reading is narrowed to something with considerably less impact. Because of the nature of tests, the texts must be short, both so that it doesn't cost too much to secure the rights and because, by abbreviating the excerpts, complexity or nuance (the base materials of critical thinking) may be sanded away.

When Close Reading Meets Standardized Response

Shel Silverstein's *The Giving Tree* tells the story of a tree that progressively provides more and more of itself to a boy the tree "loves." As the boy grows into a man he returns for the tree's apples to sell, its branches to build a house, and ultimately the trunk itself for a boat, until the tree is a stump, which the "boy," who is now an old man, finally returns to sit upon and rest. At the conclusion, reunited with the boy, the tree was once again "happy."

A standardized test question on *The Giving Tree*, working from a close reading framework, might be something like:

Which of the following words best explains the emotions of the tree?

A. Sad
B. Loving
C. Happy
D. Content
E. Selfless

The "correct" answer would be "loving" because the text explicitly says the tree "loves" the boy. "Happy" would trip up many, because it fits the conclusion of the story, but the test writers would be able to point to a line in the text that describes that tree in one moment as "happy . . . but not really."

Never mind that the best answer would be all of the above, even though "sad" is implicit, rather than explicit. Also never mind that how we see the tree may be significantly dependent on our individual response to the text. Meaning is created when reader and text intersect. Those intersections will be different for different readers.

While *The Giving Tree* is a children's story, it offers up many different avenues for response and analysis. Some see the tree as an avatar of Christ exemplifying *agape*, a love that is fulfilled through sacrifice and therefore exemplary. An objectivist like Ayn Rand, on the other hand, would find the tree's behavior absurd, and in her world view, immoral.

Others focus on the behavior of the boy as he selfishly consumes the tree's resources without a care for the tree's life; they see a parable about environmentalism.

As a child, I found the book unsettling and sad because of how thoughtlessly cruel the boy was to the tree, while others think it's beautiful and sweet because of the tree's willingness to sacrifice for the boy it loves. The contradictions and complexities are among the reasons *The Giving Tree* remains a perennial favorite. It provides something different to different readers and refuses to give up its meaning, or meanings, without significant consideration.

Reducing complex texts to multiple choice questions, and believing those questions test how closely or how well a student reads, requires a willful ignoring of some of our most important human qualities. As tests are developed, countless numbers of these compromises must be made to make sure the tests are consistent or "valid" (in the statistical sense) and can be "normed" year to year. The role of a test to assess knowledge soon becomes lost. The purpose of the test is the test itself.

When we judge a piece of writing we are inevitably bringing a set of unspoken and sometimes even unrecognized values to that judgment.

Close reading, as tested on standardized tests, often requires students to set aside any aspect of their humanity to do well. They must adopt a faux-objective mindset to suss out the answer desired by the test makers. And given what we know about systemic biases in these tests, it's reasonable to believe that some students must actively deny their own humanity to "succeed."

The belief that responses to writing can or should be standardized is, and I say this with all due respect, silly.

We Contain Multitudes

Two responses to the same book:

> . . . a wise, rueful, surprisingly tender book about what happens when we get what we want, and then what happens when we keep on wanting things. A very American novel, in other words, a novel that reminds me of Walker Percy's and Saul Bellow's very American novels. I can think of no higher praise . . .

> Awful. The plot is weak, the characters are wholly dislikable. There's little or nothing here of interest or value, and there is no real reason for anyone to read the book.[13]

The book in question is one of mine, a novel called *The Funny Man*.[14] It took me eight years to write it. I teared up when the first copy arrived at my door.

I teared up also at the very kind blurb (the first quote) provided to me by Brock Clarke, a novelist I've long admired. I teared up again when going to the Amazon page for the book and seeing that a user named "Harkius" had savaged me in a one-star review, which is reprinted in part in the second response.

So who is right? One would like to believe it's the well-regarded novelist who compares me to an actual Nobel prize winner, rather than the anonymous Amazon reviewer, but can we be so certain?

Is Mark Twain the first great truly "American" writer of classic literature that continues to resonate generation after generation, or is he a "hack writer who would not have been considered fourth rate in Europe, who tricked out a few of the old proven 'sure fire' literary skeletons with sufficient local color to intrigue the superficial and the lazy,"[15] as William Faulkner believed?

Of course, the strong consensus is that both Twain and Faulkner deserve their spots in the pantheon of American literature, but these opinions are not universal, nor should they be.

Subjective responses to writing are a feature, not a bug, and to be able to articulate the whys and wherefores of our subjective responses is an important critical thinking skill. But subjectivity is the enemy of standardization, so any exam assessing writing must somehow engineer as much subjectivity as possible out of the equation.

The result is a focus on writing that is divorced from the most pleasurable aspects of the act, deciding what you think and have to say. Instead, test takers are asked to create a simulacrum of writing.

The way this has manifested itself in high-stakes standardized exams is positively disastrous.

From 2005 to 2014—when it was altered and made optional—there was no higher-stakes writing exam than the SAT essay, an approach that largely reflects how writing prompts have been used in standardized assessments up and down the educational ladder.

The original version of the SAT essay was a timed, handwritten exam with a prompt closed in terms of topic but entirely open in terms of content; furthermore, access to outside sources and research was forbidden, making for a set of conditions under which precisely zero writers work in the real world.

An example from 2014:

Prompt 1

Think carefully about the issue presented in the following excerpt and the assignment below.

Some politicians and educators advocate teaching values and character in schools. They claim that children need guidance to develop honesty, kindness, and trustworthiness and that schools should consider it their responsibility to foster these qualities just as they aim to foster academic skills. But good character simply cannot be taught in classrooms and through textbooks. Attempts to make values part of the curriculum will only take time and resources away from important academic subjects.

Assignment: Is it wrong to try to teach values and character in the classroom? Plan and write an essay in which you develop your point of view on this issue. Support your position with reasoning and examples taken from your reading, studies, experience, or observations.[16]

The resulting writing was scored in no more than three minutes by anonymous graders hired as temporary workers who had to adhere to production quotas. Imagine Lucy and Ethel at the chocolate factory, only with students' blue books instead of bonbons.

This largely made the content of the writing itself irrelevant. In fact, to do well on the essay-writing portion of the SAT, Les Perelman, former director of MIT's Writing Across the Curriculum program and an expert in designing and evaluating writing assessments, had some advice: "Just make stuff up."

"It doesn't matter if [what you write] is true or not," Perelman said. "In fact, trying to be true will hold you back."[17]

The SAT essay exam tested students on their ability to produce a writing simulation, not on their genuine writing abilities.

The result is what I call "pseudo-academic BS," a bizarre and counterproductive style where ten-dollar words like "plethora," "myriad," and "quintessential" are sprinkled in, whether the meaning of the sentence demands it or not.

The prose sounds like a caricature of a *Masterpiece Theatre* host who has swallowed a dictionary and derives pleasure from mangling syntax. A simple recitation of a fact like "Smartphone use has increased by 43 percent among today's college students," comes out as "Recently matriculated university undergraduates engage with new touchscreen-technology phones in increasingly significant ways, which is belied by the fact that 43 percent of them now do it more." This is not an exaggeration.

When we're testing students' ability to "bullshit on demand," as Les Perelman puts it, it should not be surprising to find a disconnect between what students experience in high school and what people like me expect in college.

Students are not dumb. They are aware that these assessments are asking them to produce BS. When I confront them with evidence of the BS-ing they tend to shrug and say they thought the goal was to sound smart. On the one hand, this displays a sophisticated understanding of audience and purpose. Unfortunately, it is counterproductive to helping students actually learn to write.

Students have their rules handed down in order to pass these assessments: essays are five paragraphs long and should never contain "I," "you," or "we." Some have been told that each paragraph should be limited to five (or seven or nine) sentences, and that all concluding paragraphs must start with "In conclusion."

We see Campbell's Law at work here. Essays are to be "well-organized," so we tell students to use the five-paragraph structure and signal the conclusion with "In conclusion" because it will pass surface-level muster.

But the resulting writing does not exist outside of the demands of standardized assessment. This creates a terrible feedback loop where students are conditioned to perform writing without any real-world occasion or audience, leaving them ill prepared for the kind of writing they will do in college and beyond.

Or even before getting to college. One of the first college-oriented writing tasks students struggle with is the application essay. Confronted with prompts asking them to synthesize aspects of their character and their life experiences into an argument that proves persuasive to admissions offices means abandoning the techniques that proved successful when BS-ing through school. Malcolm Carter, a senior at Wheaton High in suburban Maryland, noted how the college essay "is nothing like the standard five-paragraph essay."

"I thought I was a good writer at first," Carter told the *Washington Post*. "I thought, I got this. But it's just not the same type of writing."[18]

A school reform regime ostensibly designed around the goal of making students "college- and career-ready" instead has the opposite effect.

The collateral damage that extends beyond stunted student-writing abilities is perhaps worse. Curiosity and creativity are explicitly punished. Being asked to write in a variety of genres and contexts is lost. Reading itself is a chore, and students are asked to decode bits that seem trivial, rather than responding to whole texts or big-picture arguments as readers do.

Add in the inevitable stress when subjected to so many tests with such apparently high stakes and it is hard to see our attempts to standardize and assess writing as anything other than counterproductive.

In fact, the thirty-plus-year focus on standardization and accountability has likely limited the amount of writing students do in school. In their comprehensive study of writing instruction in middle and high schools, Arthur Applebee and Judith Langer found that the average student was writing three to four pages of original work per week, *altogether*, across every single course. In a nine-week grading period, the average student only does two assignments requiring them to write three or more pages.[19]

Over 80 percent of students in English classes are expected to take a high-stakes test in a given year. The percent of the high-stakes exam grade based on open-ended responses (which could be as short as a single sentence) is 17.8 percent for middle school and 30.3 percent for high school. All of this concern about how much students are writing, and 70 percent of them are not even required to write, all because of the nature of these tests.

The testing also soaks up instructional time that could be better used. Charles Sampson, the superintendent of the Freehold Regional High School District in New Jersey, calculated that juniors in a New Jersey public high school will lose two full days of class to testing between mid-April and mid-June each year. This doesn't even take into account the amount of preparation associated with those high-stakes exams. "As a superintendent, I am gravely concerned. As a parent, I am outraged," he says.[20]

Kathleen Jasper, an assistant principal in a Florida high school, left her job when she could no longer stomach what she estimated to be "40 to 50 percent" of the year dedicated to testing. "I was being forced to implement bad education policy," she told NPR's education reporter, Anya Kamenetz.[21]

Teachers are tasked with preparing students for writing exams that carry significant stakes, but that also involve little writing. Those that do contain writing are done under conditions bearing little resemblance to the kinds of complicated, meaningful writing they will be asked to do in college and career.

The resulting effects on students should not be mysterious.

It is almost painful to say this, but the early part of the semester of my typical first-year writing course often involves a kind of "deprogramming" of students. I do not like to think of young humans having been programmed, but it is my experience that they are.

A common approach to writing that students will encounter in a college first-year writing course—that every piece is a custom job, created by a unique intelligence (the writer), in the service of the needs (purpose) of a specific audience—is almost entirely foreign.

Students in my courses are not starting from zero, but a good deal of the early part of the semester is spent unlearning everything they've been required to do in the past.

This is a lousy way to make students "college- and career-ready."

The Problem of Education Fads

Marshmallow Experiments and Marshmallow Tests

In 1960, Walter Mischel of Stanford University conducted the first iteration of his famous "marshmallow experiment."

In a nursery school at Stanford, Mischel put thirty-two children—sixteen boys and sixteen girls, aged four to six—one at a time in an empty room and presented them with a treat, like a marshmallow or a cookie. He told them they could eat the treat immediately, or if they waited fifteen minutes, they could get a second treat.[1]

The goal was to see what behaviors children engaged in as they attempted to delay gratification. Those who could wait for the greater reward were believed to have more self-control.

Follow-up studies showed that children who exhibited more self-control did better in school, were more likely to be described by their parents as "competent," and even had higher SAT scores.[2]

The marshmallow experiment, which was meant to observe how different children practice self-regulation, quickly became the "marshmallow test" and took root in education as a kind of holy grail of potential. If we could teach students self-control, they would grow up to be healthy, happy, successful adults. Soon, we were measuring student self-control, and grading it, and the "experiment" that had become a "test" was now subject to its own curriculum and monitoring.

Unfortunately, the nuances of what the marshmallow experiment reveals about children and behavior is lost in the shuffle. The limits of the marshmallow test as predictive of future outcomes are significant.

Follow-up studies revealed underlying complexities to children's responses to the marshmallow test. Researchers realized that in some cases the results of the marshmallow test actually reflected how often children experience adults breaking faith with children. If you live in an unstable situation and are promised future rewards that never come, you would be foolish to turn down a reward that was right in front of you.[3]

Other studies comparing children from different cultures also demonstrate the limits of this kind of experiment to tell us something meaningful and actionable. Children from the Nso community in Cameroon who live without modern conveniences such as water and electricity and who are expected to play a role in raising younger siblings "rocked" the marshmallow test as compared to children from Germany.[4]

Even Mischel laments how the marshmallow "experiment" became the marshmallow "test."[5] The initial goal was to study the "things kids did naturally to make self-control easier or harder for them." Some sang songs, some dug for gold up their noses. Others consciously articulated that their parents would be proud of them if they waited. Mischel wanted to understand how children behave, rather than developing a prescription for how all children *should* behave.

Mischel also recognized the limits of drawing broad conclusions from the "unbelievably elitist subset" of his experimental subjects, children of Stanford faculty and graduate students.[6]

None of these shortcomings stopped Mischel's marshmallow experiment from spawning legions of what is only one strain of quick-fix pedagogical approaches that have infected educational practices over the years.

The Hype Cycle

Education fads tend to follow a highly predictable hype cycle.

An interesting finding—some children from a particular background come equipped with strategies for self-distraction—

morphs into WE MUST TEACH CHILDREN SELF-CONTROL SO THEY DON'T BECOME FAILURES AND LIVE HOPELESS LIVES OF QUIET DESPERATION!

The "marshmallow test" is an ur-example of the hype cycle that happens over and over again in education:

1. Research uncovers an interesting finding that seems correlated to student "success."
2. Breathless coverage trumpets a new "revolution" in learning, which will unlock all students' potential regardless of race or economic background.
3. "Success" is defined down to something quantifiable like scores on a standardized test.
4. Very quickly, all nuances surrounding the finding are quickly washed away, so any underlying causes are pushed aside in the interest of raising scores on the test that matters above all.
5. Once the key measurement has been determined, a behaviorist approach is adopted. If students who exhibit more self-control on the marshmallow test do better on the SAT, students who demonstrate self-control are praised, and those who don't are punished, ostensibly in an effort to induce these students to practice greater self-control. We ignore that "self" is part of self-control and adopt policies and practices that require compliance, rather than developing the underlying skill.
6. The burden of implementing this new curriculum falls entirely on teachers via administrative diktat. Nothing is removed from teachers' responsibilities to make way for this additional requirement, although many things naturally fall by the wayside. Teachers are to be held accountable for how their students perform on these new metrics while being given very little if any assistance in implementing these new programs.

7. Ultimately, nothing much seems to happen. Some students improve on these new metrics; others don't. To the extent that they change it's difficult to correlate those changes to the curriculum. Basically, it's noise.
8. Enthusiasm fades, and questions arise as to whether the latest approach is sensible. Ultimately, even supporters of the initiative climb off the bandwagon, though the lack of success is almost always blamed on "poor implementation" rather than a flawed premise.
9. A new magic bullet arrives on the scene. Return to Step 1.

Educational fads come and go so quickly it's sometimes difficult to remember all of them. At one point, "learning styles"—the idea that different students learn in different ways (kinesthetic, visual, aural, and so forth)—burst like a nova before being entirely debunked.[7] The self-esteem movement took a sound principle—students do better when they believe themselves capable—and spawned entire curriculums designed to boost self-esteem. Those curriculums quickly came under fire for creating the "everyone-gets-a-trophy" generation. Large, federally led reform programs such as No Child Left Behind and Race to the Top were essentially fads, panaceas with some basis in reality, but reflecting wishful and fantastic thinking instead of being rooted in a sound research base and implemented with caution and care.

These fads distort classroom practices, particularly as they come to briefly dominate the scene. Teachers are whipsawed by new initiatives showing up out of the blue, the new seeming to erase the old, no explanation or direction offered.

Breaking the Hype Cycle

The first step to countering the boom-and-bust cycle of educational fads is to recognize that some aspects of learning will be beyond quantification. We do not seek to quantify how much we love our families or our favorite sports teams, but we know this love exists.

As sociologist William Bruce Cameron famously said, "Not everything that counts can be counted, and not everything that can be counted, counts."

Treating something like self-control as a skill to be measured and graded, and then attaching consequences to that grade, trades temporary "success" on short-term measurements for long-term change, and it ignores the vital role of intrinsic motivation in engendering meaningful and lasting development.

Love and Pleasure Beats Self-Control and Compliance

We have long known that intrinsic motivation, an internal self-directed desire to engage with a task, is a key to learning. Intrinsic motivation makes us more likely to risk failure and therefore stretch our boundaries and learn from our mistakes.

The research on this motivation is clear and has been for quite some time. Educator Alfie Kohn sounded the warning in 1993 with his book, *Punished by Rewards: The Trouble with Gold Stars, Incentive Plans, A's, Praise, and Other Bribes,* which is largely rooted in a synthesis of research conducted decades earlier.[8]

Daniel Pink further popularized the same research Kohn relies on in *Drive: The Surprising Truth about What Motivates Us.*[9] The "surprise" shouldn't have been surprising. In teacher circles, the news was old.

In packaging the findings of much of this seminal research into a consumer-friendly package, Pink argues that motivation hinges on three conditions: autonomy, mastery, and purpose.

Autonomy means having sufficient freedom to pursue our own curiosities driven by individual desires.

Mastery means we are motivated by a desire to achieve goals of our own design, and equally important, to have experiences that reinforce this desire along the way. The importance of mastery suggests the doing (process) is as important as or more important than the having done (the product).

Purpose means we believe what we are doing is important and meaningful to ourselves, to the world at large, or both.

A moment's reflection reveals the simple truth of these ideas. Any successful person has likely lived them.

In fact, reconsiderations of the marshmallow test in the fifty years since its first iteration reveal that self-control as a route to success is significantly overrated. Researchers at the University of Chicago found that when pursuing long-term goals, "the presence of immediate rewards" is more correlated with persistence than delayed gratification.[10]

In other words, if we want to keep at something over a long period of time, it must be fun and interesting along the way.

Research that led to the development of Harvard Business School professor Teresa Amabile's "progress principle" reveals that in the workplace the single most important factor for employee engagement is believing that they are "making *progress on a project that matters*."[11]

Writing is a consistently frustrating, even enervating, experience. Many times during my work on this project I considered just giving up on it. What drives me forward is not the knowledge that it will be published—indeed, I started the book long before I knew it would be published. Rather, I've continued because the process of writing the book meets the criteria articulated by Pink in *Drive*. I am allowed to write on a subject of personal fascination (autonomy). The writing of the book allows me to thread individual ideas together into a cohesive whole, and in so doing reveals additional ideas I was not previously aware of (mastery). And as I work, I believe more and more strongly that we're damaging students by subjecting them to ways of teaching that alienate them from their own selves and deep desires, and we must change these practices before more harm is done. My purpose is to undo this damage.

Inevitably, the education panacea hype cycle devolves into something representing the opposite of these traits. Autonomy is sacrificed in the name of compliance. Mastery is almost absent, as the external motivation of good grades or avoiding punishment becomes the sole reason to exhibit the desired behavior.

Purpose? Remember "I love learning; I hate school"? From the student perspective, the purpose of school is school, which means pleasing whatever assessment is currently in vogue. The result is policies and curriculum that carry a strong scent of "the beatings will continue until morale improves."

Meanwhile, underlying factors that play a much larger role in student achievement, such as poverty, remain unaddressed. The shiny object of the quick fix seems to carry much greater fascination than the heavier lift of systemic examination and change.

Gritology: Hype at Work

Recently, Mischel's "self-control" has seen a resurgence and repackaging in the form of "grit."

Grit is the domain of Dr. Angela Duckworth, a professor at the University of Pennsylvania, who defines the term this way: "Grit is passion and perseverance for very long-term goals. Grit is having stamina. Grit is sticking with your future, day in, day out, not just for the week, not just for the month, but for years, and working really hard to make that future a reality. Grit is living life like it's a marathon, not a sprint."[12]

In her research, Dr. Duckworth has discovered that those who are "grittier" (as measured by a self-reported quiz), are more successful, whether it be in mastering algebra, navigating plebe year at West Point, or maintaining a successful marriage. The potential applications to education are obvious. If children can be made grittier, they will be more likely to become successful adults.

The story of grit follows the education-fad hype cycle. Duckworth and her philosophy of grit were first widely popularized by journalist Paul Tough in his bestselling book from 2012, *How Children Succeed: Grit, Curiosity, and the Hidden Power of Character*, which yoked together various strains of behaviorist teaching and presented them as far more important to student success than intelligence or native ability.[13]

The narrative is seductive. On the surface it is egalitarian: not all of us are born with the same ability, but anyone can learn the sorts of character traits that translate to success. It also fits in with our long-standing cultural favoring of "hard work" and "stick-to-itiveness."

The hype cycle kicks in.

Angela Duckworth gets featured treatment in Tough's book, and in 2013 records a TED talk that has been viewed over twelve million times. She receives a MacArthur Foundation "Genius" Grant. She establishes her own lab at the University of Pennsylvania dedicated to studying grit.

Grit as our next panacea is off and running.

The KIPP charter schools were a willing host, already having conceived of a CPA (character point average) alongside the traditional GPA. KIPP jumped in with both feet, creating "character report cards" (later changed to "character growth cards"), which measure traits like "zest," "grit," "optimism," "self-control," "gratitude," "social intelligence," and "curiosity."[14]

Of course, it is not exactly new for one's character to be a part of what is observed and reported on for students. "Plays well with others" on a two-pronged "satisfactory" or "needs improvement" scale appeared on my grade school report card in the 1970s. Schools are social spaces, and becoming properly socialized is understood as an important function of schooling. Traditionally, we've tended to see proper socialization as a natural byproduct of putting children in social situations. Conflict will arise, but navigating that conflict will ultimately lead to social-emotional growth.

But by turning character into a quasi-academic subject through a behaviorist model—KIPP students are even encouraged to chant the word "grit" as a source of reinforcement[15]—children's characters become something to hold over their heads. Rather than creating an atmosphere where students can practice character through a process of trial and error while allowing room for autonomy, mastery, and purpose, they are cowed into compliance.

In 2016 schools in eight California districts began explicitly testing students on character traits like self-control and consideration. In theory this is meant to be a reconsideration of an approach that focuses too closely on test scores in reading and math by valuing the "whole child." These character scores would be a component of measuring student, school, and teacher performance.[16]

Unfortunately, there's a rub. As of yet, we don't know how to teach social-emotional learning skills like grit.

Who says so? Angela Duckworth.

When resigning from the group implementing the initiative in California, she said, "I do not think we should be doing this; it is a bad idea." When talking about a working paper on the difficulty of teaching social-emotional skills, Duckworth joked, "Our working title was all measures suck, and they all suck in their own way."[17]

We are now measuring and assessing students, teachers, and schools on something we don't know how to teach and even if we could teach it, we have no idea how to measure it.

Does this sound like a good idea? This is the work of the hype cycle. Even the progenitor of "grit" can't put the genie back in the bottle.

There are still other problems associated with the use of character report cards and untested social-emotional skills curriculum.

Jeffrey Aaron Snyder, professor of educational studies at Carleton College, argues that today's character-based instruction lacks a moral component and promotes an "amoral and careerist, 'looking out for number one' point of view." The reason to become gritty is to win. All character traits in KIPP's system are predicated on winning the race to the top, as opposed to other values such as working for the "common good" or becoming a better person.

Snyder says, "Today's grit and self-control are basically industry and temperance in the guise of psychological constructs rather than moral imperatives."[18] It takes tremendous grit to become a successful concert violinist, but it also takes grit to become a successful white supremacist. When people on the street are going to be compelled to punch you in the face, it takes significant self-control not to strike first and wind up in jail.

As Snyder observes, Bernie Madoff, one of the great crooks of all time, would score well on the KIPP measurements of being zestful and optimistic with extremely high social intelligence. These traits are what allowed him to maintain his con for so long.

The other problem is similar to the emphasis on standardized tests in math and reading: character education of this stripe reduces education to "college- and career-readiness." On the surface, this is an admirable goal, but when student agency and autonomy is lost in the process, not only are we preparing them poorly for the rigors of college, where resilience is not going to be enforced by teachers, we are closing off other arenas where these admirable character traits may be on display.

Most of us are gritty about something, and it may not be school *qua* school. As Snyder says, "Many of my high school friends were listless in math class but 'gritty' and 'zesty' on the basketball court or the football field."

Grit itself is a kind of tautology: the gritty display grit; therefore, grit is good. Duckworth's book, *Grit: The Power of*

Passion and Perseverance, focuses on figures like National Spelling Bee winners and Seattle Seahawks coach Pete Carroll, observing and admiring how they're able to maintain a kind of monomaniacal focus on their goals. No doubt these people have achieved great success, but there's little discussion of whether they are, for example, happy.

One gets the feeling that the grittiest people Duckworth talks to wouldn't even understand such a question. For them, being gritty is the way they interact with the world. But for many of us, this will fail to resonate.

Actor/musician Will Smith is quoted admiringly by Duckworth: "The only thing that I see that is distinctly different about me is I'm not afraid to die on a treadmill. I will not be outworked, period. You might have more talent than me, you might be smarter than me, you might be sexier than me, you might be all of those things—you got it on me in nine categories. But if we get on the treadmill together, there's two things: You're getting off first, or I'm going to die. It's really that simple. . . ."[19]

Consider this for a second. A grit-forward philosophy suggests the goal of life is to compete up to and including the point of your own death. Under this framework, grit simply becomes the ability to weather abuse, usually delivered by others, but sometimes coming from the self. Is this the kind of character we want to champion in the interests of student well-being?

In writing, while hard work and perseverance are necessary, deciding when to quit a project—I prefer the term "cutting bait"—that is not going to work is in itself a vital skill.

In 2001, Michael Chabon won the Pulitzer Prize for fiction for his novel, *The Amazing Adventures of Kavalier & Clay*. It never would have happened if he hadn't abandoned a novel called *Fountain City* years before. *Fountain City* was to be the follow-up to his highly regarded debut, *The Mysteries of Pittsburgh*, but soon he felt the book "erasing me, breaking me down, burying me alive, drowning me, kicking me down the stairs."[20] Despite years of work and hundreds of pages drafted, Chabon abandoned the book.

Knowing when to quit something that may be doing you harm is in fact a mark of maturity, one Will Smith might have benefited from while making the notorious turkey *After Earth*, with its 11 percent freshness rating on Rotten Tomatoes.[21]

There are many other ways to conceive paths to success that circumvent Duckworth's notion of grit. The research reconsidering the marshmallow test offers one direction, one where we help students practice finding their "fit" instead of emphasizing "grit" above everything else.

Most of us are not Pete Carroll, Will Smith, spelling bee champions, or other outstanding individuals who succeed through superhuman displays of grit. Why would we orient education around a trait that appears to be so rare and something potentially immutable, akin to personality traits like being introverted or extraverted?

Education researcher and activist Ira Socol argues that children from less privileged backgrounds need not "grit" but "slack." For children who must display grit in their day-to-day lives, Socol believes schools should be places of "abundance" where they can experience the kind of freedom and opportunity people from more privileged backgrounds take for granted.[22]

An insistent focus on curriculum of any stripe—be it academics or character—as the sole key to student development obscures all of the underlying factors at play regarding children's behavior and performance in school. As Socol says, some kids may have exhausted their supply of grit just making it to the school building. Others may have a hard time being zesty when they're hungry.

By falling for these fads, we fail to address root causes of gaps in opportunity and achievement.

Paul Tough, the most important early popularizer of grit, agrees with me.

Helping Children Succeed

In 2016, Tough published the much less heralded follow-up to *How Children Succeed*, titled *Helping Children Succeed: What Works and Why*.[23] Through his reporting on character-based curriculum and approaches, Tough couldn't help but notice what was already known: in many cases, focusing on teaching social-emotional skills like grit seemed to have little impact on achievement.

Tough's *Helping Children Succeed* essentially reversed the position he had espoused earlier. From the jacket copy: "Rather than trying to 'teach' skills like grit and self-control, [Tough] argues, we should focus instead on creating the kinds of environments, both at home and at school, in which those qualities are most likely to flourish."

Tough claims the book is based on the latest neuroscience and cognitive research, suggesting that these findings were discovered after he wrote his first book, but in fact many of the issues he presents have been known for decades. Research on the effects of stress on IQ date to the 1980s.

The hypothesis linking lead in the air and decreased educational achievement and increased violence was published in the early part of the millennium.

The National School Lunch Program, in recognition of the importance of nutrition in learning, was established by a congressional act and signed into law by President Harry S. Truman in 1946.

The intersection of nutrition and educational achievement was subjected to a meta-analysis as early as 1984.[24]

Our willingness to embrace these fads reflects a deep desire to do better by students we know we are failing. By lurching from one fad to another, though, we fail to address the more entrenched underlying conditions that are having a far greater impact on students.[25]

Sadly, there is a new source of hype that is threatening to take over education: technology.

The Problem of Technology Hype
Making Teachers Obsolete Any Day Now

....

In 1913 Thomas Edison declared to the *New York Dramatic Mirror*, "Books will soon be obsolete in the public schools. Scholars will be instructed through the eye. It is possible to teach every branch of human knowledge with the motion picture. Our school system will be completely changed in ten years."[1]

In 1953 behavioral psychologist B. F. Skinner, best known for his work with rats and pigeons, developed what is (erroneously) called the first "teaching machine." Skinner said, "There is no reason the school should be any less mechanized . . . than the kitchen." A 1962 story in *Popular Science* predicted that half of all students would be using a Skinner teaching machine by 1965.[2]

In 2012 Sebastian Thrun, Stanford professor and co-founder of massive open online course (MOOC) provider Udacity, declared that "in 50 years, there will be only 10 institutions in the world delivering higher education."[3]

Also in 2012 Thrun was honored with a *Smithsonian* magazine American Ingenuity Award for Education.[4] The revolution was afoot. In short order how we learn would be radically transformed.

And yet, somehow, only a year later, Sebastian Thrun was declaring his own company's product "lousy" as he pivoted away from undergraduate education to finely targeted corporate training.[5]

By 2017 Udacity vice president Clarissa Shen was pronouncing MOOCs "dead."[6]

From transforming higher education to "dead" in five years. Like education fads such as "grit," technological solutions to the problems of education follow a familiar cycle of hype, boom (sort of), and bust.

The reasons MOOCs failed to transform education should seem obvious. Completing an online course in which you're enrolled with thirty thousand of your closest friends working on an asynchronous timeline requires a kind of self-discipline and self-direction few of us are able to achieve. Stripped of social interaction, students become passive consumers of content (usually videos) they are expected to absorb and then regurgitate onto assessments (almost always multiple choice).[7] MOOCs mimic the worst aspects of large lecture "sage-on-a-stage" models, but that didn't stop credulous social commentators such as *New York Times* columnist Thomas Friedman from marveling at their potential. "How can colleges charge $50,000 a year if my kid can learn it all free from massive open online courses?" Friedman asked, in a paean to the coming MOOC revolution a mere eight months before Thrun himself declared Udacity's MOOCs a "lousy product."[8]

It turns out Thomas Friedman's kid is unlikely to learn much from massive open online courses, because MOOC completion rates rarely go higher than 15 percent and often cluster around 5 percent.[9] Thomas Friedman's daughters also already earned their undergraduate degrees at Yale and Williams. I wonder if he regrets not having the chance to send them to an entirely online experience instead of those elite institutions.[10]

The early MOOC boosters like Thrun and Anant Agarwal of EdX, another MOOC provider, championed MOOCs as, in Agarwal's words, "borderless, gender-blind, race-blind, class-blind and bank account-blind."[11] However, MOOCs in practice prove to be anything but. The most likely completers of MOOC courses are those who already have post-secondary degrees,[12] because MOOCs are suited to what sociologist Tressie McMillan Cottom calls "roaming autodidacts . . . a self-motivated, able learner that is simultaneously embedded in technocratic futures *and* disembedded from place, cultur[e], history, and markets."[13]

MOOCs as a disruptive solution require us to imagine learners as a sort of null state without ethnicity, culture, or background. MOOCs employ a one-size-fits-all pedagogy, in which there must be a "best" teacher of calculus, of plant biology, of art history. If we can just identify those people, we can create courses that allow "everyone" to learn.

Or even better, we don't need master professors, but celebrities, because they are compelling and telegenic. When MOOCs were still in their initial hype phase, Anant Agarwal of EdX said, "From what I hear, really good actors can actually teach really well. So just imagine, maybe we get Matt Damon to teach Thévenin's theorem. I think students would enjoy that more than taking it from Agarwal."[14]

Thrun, Agarwal, Friedman, Skinner, Edison—all make the same categorical error in their belief that technology can transform "education" by reducing education to mere content delivery. If exposure to content were all it took to learn, Edison would have been correct about the impact of the moving picture in 1913, and we wouldn't have been subjected to the serial predictions of the transformation of education that seem to follow each introduction of new technology.

While the novelty of Matt Damon explaining concepts related to circuits and electronics may draw eyeballs and offer "entertainment," education requires something deeper: "engagement."

Students must opt in to the experience, which requires more than a handsome face and a smooth presentation.

Technological solutions to the problems of learning value a "frictionless" experience, but we shouldn't forget that friction makes heat and heat is energy. As Bernard Fryshman, a professor of physics with fifty years of experience, says, one of faculties' most important roles is to "jostle students into active learning."[15]

Experiences, Not Information

In fact, contact with faculty and between students may be the most meaningful part of education. The 2014 "Great Jobs Great Lives" Purdue-Gallup survey of more than thirty thousand college graduates across the United States found that the *experience* of college was most important when it came to being more engaged in the work.[16]

As the data shows, the relationships between students and professors play a key role in future work engagement. For each affirmative answer to the following conditions, students are twice as likely to be engaged in their jobs:

- I had a mentor who encouraged me to pursue my goals and dreams.
- I had at least one professor who made me excited about learning.
- My professors cared about me as a person.

Engagement at work is particularly important because it plays such an outsized role when it comes to one's overall "well-being." Someone who is engaged at work is over four and a half times more likely to be "thriving" when it comes to well-being.

This chain of happiness, education to career to overall well-being, is built on human relationships, relationships that are not possible under distance learning models such as MOOCs.

Despite the rapid and spectacular flameout of MOOCs in transforming education, we are in the midst of a new fad in an earlier part of the hype cycle: "personalized learning."

Our Newest Hype

The term "personalized learning" crops up in a lot of different contexts and has roots in the progressive education movement (think Maria Montessori and John Dewey), but in the ed tech product realm, we're talking about something called "adaptive software."

While there are wrinkles and variations, the concept of adaptive software generally goes like this: As students work through a set of problems, the software identifies the point of "failure" where the student no longer appears to understand the material. Once the precise nature of the student's knowledge is identified, the software can deliver targeted "lessons" (usually videos) to help fill the gaps, after which the student is retested on the material. Rinse and repeat until the student answers the questions correctly.

In theory, adaptive software allows students to receive lessons customized to their needs and abilities, just-in-time interventions mediated by algorithms collecting data on the behaviors of thousands or even millions of other students.

Jose Ferreira, former CEO of Knewton, an ed tech company focused on "personalized learning," told NPR in 2015 that his software is "like a robot tutor in the sky that can semi-read your mind and figure out what your strengths and weaknesses are, down to the percentile."[17]

Bill Gates and Mark Zuckerberg, who between them have invested close to $20 billion in education, are both fans of personalized learning in the form of adaptive software. In 2017, Bill Gates announced his intention to invest an additional $1.7 billion in education, 60 percent of which will be targeted toward the "development of new curricula," which is likely to include adaptive software.[18]

The Chan Zuckerberg Initiative, funded by Mark Zuckerberg's Facebook wealth and run by his wife, Priscilla Chan, has over $60 billion in assets and in the education realm is heavily focused on personalized learning delivered via adaptive software.[19]

The Summit Denali charter school in Sunnyvale, CA, which has been quasi-adopted by Chan Zuckerberg, has incorporated software developed by Facebook into many of their day-to-day school activities.[20]

Given the billions of dollars that are about to be invested in algorithm-driven software labeled as "personalized learning," it's worth asking: Does it work?

Who knows? Maybe? On some things? It depends? What do you mean by "work" exactly?

When students who spend time interacting with algorithmic learning are tested on assessments driven by algorithmic learning, some boost in "achievement" can be observed.

Of course, if you spend hours upon hours playing *Candy Crush* you will also get very good at *Candy Crush*. Whether your *Candy Crush* skill translates beyond the game is a different question. Often with adaptive software, it is the students who adapt to the algorithm in order to please the programming, rather than the other way around.

Adaptive-learning algorithms are not neutral, unbiased "teaching machines," and contra Jose Ferreira, they do not read minds. These algorithms aggregate responses and present canned content. If a student consistently misses a question on something like cell division, the algorithm will call up the mini-lesson on cell division over and over again until the student successfully answers the (always multiple choice) question about cell division.

Is repeating the same presentation over and over word for word to confused students a pedagogical practice we would accept in a human instructor? Surely not, and yet it is trotted out as an upside to software-driven adaptive learning, an indefatigable robo-tutor willing to repeat itself over and over until the student "learns."

What is it we think students may "learn" in these systems?

But Seriously, Does It Work?

To the extent one finds scores on standardized assessments meaningful—and we've already seen why we should be skeptical of thinking this—perhaps personalized learning shows some extremely limited promise. A Rand Corporation report on the effectiveness of personalized learning—funded by the Bill & Melinda Gates Foundation—finds some gains in math and reading scores.[21]

At the same time, John F. Pane, senior scientist at Rand, says of personalized education, "The evidence base is very weak at this point."[22]

Furthermore, Doug Levin, an education technology consultant, noticed an interesting finding from the same report. Students in personalized learning programs (which are overwhelmingly tech-oriented) enjoy school less, feel less comfortable in school, are less likely to feel safe in school, and are less likely to say there is an adult in school who knows them well.[23]

We should not be surprised that a school day could be alienating when it's dominated by interacting with a screen and a computer running software specifically designed to highlight your deficiencies. Being inspired or mentored by a teacher will be a thing of the past when algorithms dominate instruction.

We already have a curiosity crisis in schools, causing students to become actively disengaged from school itself. Personalized learning of the kind favored by Gates, Zuckerberg, and other education disruptors only promises to make this disengagement worse.

Already Flaming Out

The real-life experiments in software-driven personalized learning seem to implode almost upon launch. AltSchool, the vision of former Google "Head of Personalization" Max Ventilla, was sent forth with $175 million in Silicon Valley seed money, including funding from Mark Zuckerberg. Nine schools were opened, boasting all manner of technological gewgaws. Ventilla had zero experience in education, but he was convinced he could "revolutionize" school. As reported by *Bloomberg Technology*,

Five years after opening, the for-profit venture has yet to solve a basic business equation. Despite charging about $30,000 for tuition, AltSchool's losses are piling up as it spends at a pace of about $40 million per year. The San Francisco company is now scaling back its ambitions for opening elementary schools around the U.S. and will instead close at least one location. In an interview, Ventilla said it's all part of the plan. The startup is shifting its focus to selling technology to other schools, a business which has struggled to date but that he said has a more promising future.[24]

Parents of children who attended the shuttered AltSchool were left in the lurch in the middle of the school year. To the extent AltSchool was successful, most parents credited a low faculty-student ratio and attentive staff, the kinds of conditions we would expect for any private school charging $30,000 a year in tuition.

And what about Jose Ferreira and his magical "robo-tutor?" How's that coming? Two years after making his boast to NPR's *Morning Edition*, Ferreira was replaced as CEO as the company "hit the reset button." Brian Kibby, Ferreira's replacement, declared that the original Knewton approach was "flawed."[25]

Every time one of these speculative forays into a tech-driven education "revolution" pivots or reboots or simply ceases to exist, students are harmed in real and significant ways.

How many generations of casualties will we accept as we search for the next tech-driven silver bullet?

Wrong Assumptions

Larry Berger, CEO of personalized learning software developer Amplify, is widely considered a pioneer in the field. Prior to leading Amplify, he co-founded Wireless Generation, which was absorbed into Amplify in a complicated 2011 deal with Amplify's initial backer, Rupert Murdoch's News Corporation.

Amplify was a kind of joint venture of egos, combining Murdoch with former New York City schools chancellor

Joel Klein, who was convinced technology could be a differentiator in education. Amplify intended to develop both hardware (an iPad-like tablet) and software that could be sold into school systems as a package. Wireless Generation would be the backbone of the software.[26]

As a business, Amplify proved to be a disaster. Hamstrung by big expenses—like Klein's $4.5 million salary—and unreasonable growth expectations, News Corp sunk more than $1 billion into the company before abandoning the tablet and transferring what remained to a team of investors in 2015, with Larry Berger leading the company, which exists in a somewhat different form today.

The financial implosion and near death of an education technology startup is entirely unsurprising. Even a sound product may have a hard time penetrating a difficult and diffuse market like education.

But in writing to Rick Hess of the American Enterprise Institute in early 2018, Larry Berger questions the very foundations of personalized learning, saying, "Until a few years ago, I was a great believer in what might be called the 'engineering' model of personalized learning, which is what most people mean by personalized learning."[27]

Berger describes the concept of personalized learning as starting with what you think kids need to learn, "measuring" the kids to place them on a "map," where everything they know is behind them, and "everything in front of them is what they need to learn next."

From the array of "learning objects" the algorithm will select a lesson, the child will complete it, they will be retested ("measured") again. If they pass the measurement, they move on. If not, they try again with something "simpler."

Berger once believed that if this process was used by "millions of kids" the "algorithms would get smarter and smarter, and make better, more personalized choices about which things to put in front of kids."

Berger confesses he spent "a decade" believing in this model, but "Here's the problem: The map doesn't exist, the measurement is impossible, and we have, collectively, built only 5% of the library."

Bill Gates and Mark Zuckerberg are preparing to invest hundreds of millions of dollars in an approach to learning that we know to be fundamentally flawed. If the apparent shortcomings of the engineering approach were not sufficient, Berger has a final admission: "As if it were not enough of a problem that this is a system whose parts don't exist, there's a more fundamental breakdown: Just because the algorithms want a kid to learn the next thing doesn't mean that a real kid actually wants to learn the thing."

Larry Berger ends his "confession" with a question, a good one: "What did your best teachers and coaches do for you—without the benefit of maps, algorithms, or data—to personalize your learning?"

The progressive education roots of "personalized education" expressed a need for students to practice personal agency in the context of their schooling. The idea was not to customize lessons for students, but for students to customize the lessons for themselves. The original conception of personalized education also emphasized the social aspect of learning, something inevitably lost when personalized learning means directing students to screens and software.

The driving value of all of these teaching machines is "efficiency," but it is difficult to reconcile the value of "efficiency" with learning. Education is an ongoing process, not a product, and what we learn as we stumble off the path is often more valuable than when we are toeing the line. Do we value "efficiency" in our relationships with our families? Is our most profound love "efficient?"

Believers in technology's potential to unlock learning often trumpet tech as a way to "free up" teachers for the work that matters, but more often algorithmic instruction serves to separate students and instructors. This is nowhere more evident than in the push for automated grading.

Automated Grading: A Very Dark Future

If an essay is written and no one is there to read it can it be considered an act of communication?

In 2013, amid the highest fever of the MOOC hype, the *New York Times* invited readers: "Imagine taking a college exam, and, instead of handing in a blue book and getting a grade from a professor a few weeks later, clicking the 'send' button when you are done and receiving a grade back instantly, your essay scored by a software program. And then, instead of being done with that exam, imagine that the system would immediately let you rewrite the test to try to improve your grade."[28]

This was the vision of EdX's Anant Agarwal for his company's automated writing assessment tool. The tool is "trained" by human graders assigning scores to responses to a given prompt; then, using the algorithmic secret sauce, the program "trains itself" to grade student responses "automatically and almost instantaneously."

In 2013, Agarwal believed the algorithm compared favorably to human graders. "This is machine learning and there is a long way to go, but it's good enough and the upside is huge," he said. "We found that the quality of the grading is similar to the variation you find from instructor to instructor."

The first problem (among many), though: computers can't read.

Computers, no matter how powerful their algorithms, can only count. The grading software very quickly compares the submitted essay to the human graded ones, measuring things like word choice, structure, and other content-independent traits.

Imagine the BS it's possible to pass by a human grader tasked with scoring a standardized exam essay in three minutes or less and multiply it by a thousand. In fact, Les Perelman of MIT has done just this, inventing the Basic Automated BS Essay Language Generator, or BABEL Generator.

Perelman's BABEL Generator is capable of spinning out sentences such as this: "Privateness has not been and undoubtedly never will be lauded, precarious, and decent. Humankind will always subjugate privateness."

Babble indeed, but when tested against the algorithmic grading product used as a backup to the human scorer on the Graduate Management Admission Test (GMAT), Perelman's BABEL Generator babble was scored a 5.4 out of 6 and was marked especially high for language use and style.[29]

As with other education technological interventions in teaching, the explicit rationale for algorithmic grading of writing is not its quality—even its biggest boosters admit its limitations—but its efficiency. However, rather than promoting algorithmic grading as a replacement for teachers, they claim outsourcing grading to software will free teachers to "pay attention to the important stuff."

But here's the thing: when it comes to teaching and learning writing, it's *all* important stuff.

What Really Happens When We "Grade"

In fact, the least important feedback is the one thing algorithmic grading software can kind of do: attach a score to piece of writing.

In genuine writing assessment, the instructor is simultaneously judging the work against all the qualities we expect in a piece of writing—content, coherence, style, correctness—while also looking for evidence of causes when some aspect of the writing seems awry. It is an act no algorithm could hope to replicate.

For example, consider a basic assignment in a college first-year writing course: an article summary. The goal is for the student to read the argument of another writer, and then distill that argument to its essence while hewing as closely to the original writer's meaning as possible. If a writer cannot accurately convey the ideas of others, they will not be able to use those ideas to shape their own expression.

The students I have worked with over the years often struggle with this assignment. In their previous experiences, many of them have been asked to prove comprehension at the level of "I have read and genuinely understood the broad subject of this article." They have rarely been required to distill or synthesize an argument to its essence, a higher order task than mere comprehension. They are comfortable repeating what they've heard/read but less experienced in articulating what a text "means."

The "close reading" featured in standardized reading assessments doesn't help much, as those questions often ask students to zoom in on individual bits and pieces at the sentence level and the effects or meaning of those bits and pieces independent of the larger argument. Put another way, they've spent a lot of time examining trees without being required to describe the forest.

Student difficulties with argument summary tend to cluster around a few common issues.

Some paraphrase rather than summarize, essentially repeating the original piece idea to idea in the order of appearance. Ideally, a summary should be significantly shorter than the original—it is meant to be an aid to understanding for those who do not know the text being summarized—so a line-by-line paraphrase doesn't work. I often restrict students' first attempt at summary to three hundred or so words, significantly shorter than what they're summarizing. Some students hit the word count having dealt with only the first few paragraphs. Having been conditioned to locate their thesis at the end of the first paragraph, they sometimes assume the same is true of all writing, but in much of the more sophisticated texts they'll read in a typical first-year writing course, the thesis may be implied rather than explicit.

Some students looking for a thesis to summarize search for a sentence to extract and quote, but not finding it, they settle for something they know isn't right, believing they should do what they've done before anyway.

Other students simply get the argument wrong. They summarize a nonexistent claim.

Another common error is what I think of as the "Spinal Tap," inspired by the scene in the film *This Is Spinal Tap*, when Nigel Tufnel (played by Christopher Guest) shows his custom Marshall amp to the documentary director Marty DiBergi (played by Rob Reiner). Tufnel is proud that, unlike other amps where the dials stop at 10, "these go to 11."

"What we do, if we need that extra push over the cliff, you know what we do . . . 11 . . . one louder."

When employing the "Spinal Tap" in a summary, the student generally gets the original argument, but then inflates it in a this-one-goes-to-eleven fashion, often through the injection of pseudo-academic BS. Something the original author found troubling is suddenly catastrophic. Something merely positive is now transcendent and life-changing.

This is an effective strategy in standardized writing assessments where the performance of erudition is more important than genuine communication, but it is ineffective when seeking to convey someone else's argument with scrupulous accuracy.

It is an easy matter to identify the areas where a summary is "wrong," where an idea is skewed or even missed entirely. I will write marginal comments such as "Is this true?" or "I don't think this is accurate." When the pseudo-academic BS gets especially thick, turned up past eleven, all the way to twelve, I may throw in a "Huh?"

But the far more important part of the work is my trying to figure out *why* the error has been made so I can offer something to the student that allows them to return to their writing process in order to do better next time. Often, this is only achieved in consultation with the students themselves. I will have a theory about what is going on, but I must test this theory against the student's own understanding.

If a student has missed the argument by a good margin, we may have a reading comprehension issue; they simply didn't understand the text to begin with.

But the roots of the issue can vary. In some cases we may be talking about lack of interest: the student couldn't get into it enough to care. In others it might be a problem of vocabulary or unfamiliar terminology, where the student's existing knowledge wasn't sufficient. I have seen this happen when a student didn't understand the meaning of a single word, essentially inferring the opposite of what was intended. In still others it might be a writing process problem: the student put off doing the assignment until the morning it was due. They turned in a first draft in which they figured things out by the end of the effort but didn't leave themselves enough time to rework the text.

The same error on the assignment may require different interventions for each student, depending on the cause. The uninterested student may need a combination of a little tough love and some help in finding ways into seemingly uninteresting texts.

The student who lacked background on the subject needs help on a process of active reading, where they act to identify their own gaps of knowledge and fill them in with additional, lateral reading. I may model this behavior for the student through my own practice.

The student with the bad process needs no intervention, provided they own up to the consequences of trying to pull off the impossible.

The peddler of pseudo-academic BS is usually practicing what was praised. For these students, we have a discussion about the different values underlying academic writing in college, the difference between communicating an idea and trying to pass an assessment where "looking smart" may be valued.

I could go on and on. Figuring out where writing has gone wrong and why is an endlessly fascinating puzzle. In order to work with student writers, the writing teacher needs access to all aspects of the student writing process. This doesn't mean we must comment on every last thing students do, but no part of the process should be hidden behind algorithmic response.

Asking writing instructors to work with students when you haven't read and assessed their writing is like asking a football coach to work with a team when the coach knows the score but hasn't watched the game.

There are other problems associated with algorithmic feedback for writing. The champions of algorithms boast about how the feedback is "instant," but we know that an important part of the writing process is extended thinking and contemplation, some of which clearly happens subconsciously over time. Every writer has put down a piece feeling stymied, only to return to it a day or a week or a year later—and suddenly the solution to the previously intractable problem has appeared.

Instant feedback can create a dependence on that feedback, feedback that often is not forthcoming in the wider world. One of the consistent frustrations my students have with my teaching style is a tendency to answer their questions with questions that point them back toward their own writing. I aim to be a sounding board, but ultimately if they are going to learn to write, they must engage in the struggle themselves.

There is a final reason we should not accept algorithmic responses to student writing, and really it could be the first or only reason.

We should not ask students to write anything that will not be read. When the chief problems of education are alienation, lack of engagement, and anxiety, where is the value in making students talk to black boxes that count in 0's and 1's?

Writing is fundamentally about communication, and when students are communicating something, the least we can do is listen.

The Problem of Folklore

....

Diagramming Sentences

To her face we called her Mrs. Thompson, but behind her back it was "Sarge."

Sarge was our eighth grade Language Arts teacher. Rumor was she'd been in the military, probably something like an officer in the Women's Air Corps, but in our imagination, she'd actually been part of the Normandy invasion, charging the beach with a knife in her teeth. Her necklace of Nazi ears was probably stored away in her top desk drawer.

No one knew the full truth. The legend grew with each successive school year.

Sarge was squat with a short, salt-and-pepper bristly haircut, and an authoritative, gravelly voice. Think R. Lee Ermey's drill sergeant in *Full Metal Jacket*.

Mrs. Thompson was old-school, and old-school teachers loved to diagram sentences, and so diagram sentences we did.

Subject, verb, direct object, indirect object, gerund, participle, independent and dependent clauses—we covered them all, over and over.

Mrs. Thompson was an important influence on my eventual path toward becoming a writer.

That influence had nothing to do with diagramming sentences.

Common Folklore

How many spaces belong after a period at the end of a sentence?

Your answer likely depends on a number of factors: your age, where and when you learned this bit of knowledge, how old the person who first conveyed this bit of knowledge was when they first learned it, your profession, how often and in what way you use word processing tools.

The answer is one. With some very limited exceptions, only one space follows the end of a sentence. Some of you are disbelieving. Some of you, like me, were taught that two spaces belong after a period, and we have had to unlearn it. Some of you may even be angry, having heard this "one space" nonsense before and declaring they will pry your second space out of your cold dead hands.

Still, regardless, the answer is one.

In the typewriter age, when Courier, a "monospace" font— meaning every letter is the same width—was dominant, two spaces after a period did help with document readability. But we don't use typewriters anymore and variable-width fonts are now the norm. In fact, in most digital mediums, like text messaging, blogging platforms, or online comments, it's impossible to put two spaces after a period—the program deletes any extras without a care.

Double-spacing after a period is an example of educational folklore, a bit of "knowledge" passed down by an authority and absorbed and accepted, initially through some sort of threat requiring compliance (points off!), to later become "the way things are."

From the student perspective, a lot of what happens in school takes the form of folklore. The assumption seems to be: if it's school, if it comes from a teacher, it's important.

Folklore is incredibly powerful. Some of you are still angry at me and will insist that I am wrong about one space after a sentence, even though just about everything you read just about everywhere uses only one space after a sentence. We cling to that which we know fiercely, and often for good reason.

But clinging to folklore when it is proven to be wrong or misguided can be very damaging.

There is much educational folklore regarding writing. Unfortunately, this folklore often prevents us from having a more productive conversation about what and how students should learn.

I was in Mrs. Thompson's classroom in 1984, ancient history. I did not thrive at diagramming sentences. I learned enough to fake it, but I could never figure out how the geometric lines on the chalkboard or in my notebook related to what I loved to read or tried to write. But diagramming sentences is part of school, so it must be important.

It turns out, not so much. There is no demonstrable link between being able to diagram sentences and being able to write effectively. This fact was codified by the National Council of Teachers of English in 1963, seven years before I was even born.

Based on a review of available research they declared, "The teaching of formal grammar has a negligible or, because it usually replaces some instruction and practice in composition, even a harmful effect on the improvement of writing."[1]

This finding was reaffirmed in 1985 in a formal resolution:

Resolved, that the National Council of Teachers of English affirm the position that the use of isolated grammar and usage exercises not supported by theory and research is a deterrent to the improvement of students' speaking and writing and that, in order to improve both of these, class time at all levels must be devoted to opportunities for meaningful listening, speaking, reading, and writing; and that NCTE urge the discontinuance of testing practices that encourage the teaching of grammar rather than English language arts instruction.[2]

The particular power of the folklore surrounding the teaching of "grammar" is significant. Some of you right now are disbelieving the NCTE's resolution (just as you disbelieve the one-space-after-a-period matter), even though it is based on a meta-analysis of dozens of studies seeking to measure the impact of different pedagogical strategies on helping students learn to write.

The post hoc fallacy (since B followed A, A must have caused B) is particularly prevalent in education. Those of us who believe ourselves to have been successfully educated must have been exposed to effective educational practices.

It is hard to think of the grammar worksheets and drills we churned through as schoolchildren being either not helpful or possibly even harmful. We don't want to believe our time was wasted, but the research is clear and has been for some time.

Because the impulse to do to others what has been done to us (for both good and ill) is so powerful, the folklore becomes entrenched. Knowledge of the ineffectiveness of direct grammar instruction was well known as far back as the 1940s. Lou LaBrant, a high school teacher/researcher, wrote in a 1946 edition of *The English Journal*, "We have some hundreds of studies now which demonstrate that there is little correlation (whatever that may cover) between exercises in punctuation and sentence structure and the tendency to use the principles illustrated in independent writing."[3]

The argument is not that grammar and effective expression are unimportant; they are hugely important. It's just that we know, beyond any doubt, that teaching them in isolation is not a useful strategy for helping students learn to write.

I wish I'd known this sooner, but like a lot of teachers, for many years I followed the folklore. I assigned grammar worksheets. I drilled students on comma usage. I picked every last nit on their drafts. But the overall quality of their writing remained unchanged. Now I know why.

Or consider this, for those of us who were subjected to sentence diagramming or drills on grammar and mechanics: How much of that information do you retain? Maybe I should be ashamed to admit this, but as I sit today, I could craft only the most rudimentary sentence diagrams. My specific knowledge of grammar beyond the basics is almost entirely gone, despite having taught a lab section dedicated to grammar for three years of graduate school. I retain more from the *Schoolhouse Rock!* grammar videos ("Verb! That's what's happenin'"; "Conjunction junction, what's your function?") of my youth than anything I recall from school itself.

Those who hold on to the notion that students must learn the "basics" of grammar before allowing writers to move on to the more difficult work of expressing ideas are denying those students access to the experiences that make us want to learn to write. It is the equivalent of music students being confined to the study of sheet music, without ever being allowed to play an actual instrument.

One three-year study covering students from ninth to eleventh grade divided students into three groups. One group experienced traditional, isolated grammar instruction, another experienced alternative grammar instruction, and the third had no formal grammar instruction, instead substituting additional reading and creative writing.

The result? In terms of writing skills, there were no significant differences among the groups. Unfortunately, the two groups who studied grammar walked away hating English.[4]

How do we expect students to improve at something they hate?

The teaching of writing, like the teaching of anything, requires a prioritization of values. What is most important at a given part of the process? What conditions and experiences help learners improve and make them eager to keep coming back to learn more?

The folklore of the direct instruction of grammar values "correctness" above all, a correctness enforced for reasons that often seem arbitrary to students, rules disconnected from any purpose other than the fact that they are handed down by an authority with the power to determine a grade.

And so the rules must be followed, generation after generation.

Unfortunately, we make many sacrifices on the altar of correctness, a practice that is surely exacerbated by testing and accountability systems that promulgate the illusion that there are right and wrong answers in the realm of reading and writing.

There are reasons why we don't keep score and everyone gets in the game when children first start playing a sport. Even parental pride doesn't turn the grade school band recital into a performance of the New York Philharmonic, and yet the audience still gives a standing ovation. Correctness is not a concern.

Back on the practice field or in the lesson room we will point out the areas for possible improvement and strategize to correct those deficiencies, but we would never consider leading our critique with all the things that were done wrong.

As adults we wouldn't tolerate such an approach if it were taken with us. When I submit this manuscript, my editor will spend a couple of pages telling me about all the wonderful things I've done before addressing the areas that need work. He will not be concerned about the many typos or imperfect sentences, knowing that we have time to work out those kinks.

The consequences of clinging to the folklore of needing to teach the grammar "basics" are significant. Michelle Navarre Cleary, a writer and writing teacher who spent years in an urban community college with a significant dropout rate, reports the effect of insisting on "correctness," saying of her students, "I have found over and over again that they overedit themselves from the moment they sit down to write. They report thoughts like 'Is this right? Is that right?' and 'Oh my god, if I write a contraction, I'm going to flunk.' Focused on being correct, they never give themselves a chance to explore their ideas or ways of expressing those ideas."[5]

Correctness is simply not a value any working writer would

even recognize as important. Joan Didion, one of the greatest prose stylists of the last fifty years, says: "Grammar is a piano I play by ear, since I seem to have been out of school the year the rules were mentioned. All I know about grammar is its infinite power. To shift the structure of a sentence alters the meaning of that sentence, as definitely and inflexibly as the position of a camera alters the meaning of the object photographed."[6]

This is not a declaration that anything goes or that students do not need to be instructed on writing good sentences, but from their earliest attempts at writing we must allow students to see that "proper" expression is dependent on audience and occasion, and this means they must make informed choices.

Right now we should be worried that Mrs. Thompson, a longtime outstanding English teacher at a highly regarded junior high school in a prosperous Chicago suburb, was teaching outdated pedagogy in 1984.

We should be even more worried that I was teaching similar methods in the mid-90s as a graduate student, or that many today continue to cling to this folklore of correctness. To get beyond the folklore we have to re-ask fundamental questions and see if we come up with different answers.

When Larry Berger of Amplify wonders, "What did your best teachers and coaches do for you—without the benefit of maps, algorithms, or data—to personalize your learning?" I think of Mrs. Thompson, not because of the sentence diagramming, but because of something much more important: she believed in me.

Learning You Have Something to Say

While Language Arts did involve lots of boring grammar exercises and sentence diagramming, we also did all kinds of different writing, including creative writing, and for Mrs. Thompson I produced my first novella.

I don't remember the title, but the main characters were the Bagelsons, a family of sentient bagels, except for the youngest Bagelson child, who was instead shaped like a bialy and was therefore something of an outcast.

I'm pretty sure I was inspired by the absurdist humor of Douglas Adams's *The Hitchhiker's Guide to the Galaxy*. I do recall lots of bread puns and the futile dream of one of the Bagelson children, who wanted to be a goalie on the soccer team. (The other team kept shooting the ball through the hole in his middle.) Daughter Bagelson was never sure if the boys liked her for her or because she was delicious tasting. The assignment was to write a story, not a novella, but I became so enamored of the world I was creating that I could not stop myself at the prescribed length.

I'm sure it was idiotic, and I should be grateful the evidence does not survive, but I remember Mrs. Thompson's comments peppering the margins: "Ha!" and "Very funny!"

When she handed it back—and I remember this because it was so meaningful—she put her hand on my shoulder and said, "I've never read anything like this."

(She meant it in a nice way.)

In the short term, this encouraging response had the unfortunate consequence of my shooting for "I've never read anything like this" on all of my assignments, an approach that is not always appropriate or conducive to good grades.

On the other hand, Mrs. Thompson had helped me understand what was important to me and that pleasing myself could be a route to having an impact on others. She is in a long line of teachers in my formative school years who—to put it plainly—cared about me as "me."

The time we spent diagramming sentences was not helpful, but my entire spirit was not sacrificed on the altar of correctness. I was allowed to be a little bit strange. I was allowed to practice the choices writers make.

Unfortunately, education folklore, largely clustered around getting students to write in the "correct" manner, persists. The pull of "it worked for me, so it must work for others" is strong, but we rarely pause to look at what was really working.

As contentious as teaching writing seems, people outside the field are often surprised by how much agreement exists among those who deeply study the discipline. We will talk more about this later.

First, we have to agree to no longer rely on folklore for our answers.

Just because the folklore says something is true doesn't make it so. I think we should challenge the folklore every chance we get. We can do better than perpetuate the cycle of folklore by handing students rules and prescriptions for writing designed to pass assessments that hold little meaning in the wider world and no connection to students' lives.

Every student should be armed with the skills to remake the world for themselves, a world rooted in their own values and desires. This requires a far more challenging approach to writing than what might be found in the folklore of grammar exercises and sentence diagramming.

Everything should be up for questioning.

The Problem of Precarity

A Difficult Admission

A game.

It's called "Guess My Salary." It's a terrible game, and I do not want to play, but it is useful, particularly for those who work outside of higher education.

The years are 2006 to 2011. My title is "lecturer" in English at Clemson University. I teach four classes every semester, a mix of writing and literature, totaling between eighty and one hundred twenty students, depending on the semester and the mix of classes.

"Professors" at the school have a two-course-per-semester load. As part of their duties, they're also expected to publish research, something I have been doing as well, but something that is not a formal part of my job responsibilities. This is a full-time job, teaching college—forty hours of work per week minimum.

But I was not a professor. Instead, I was a contingent instructor, a member of the "precariat," a group that labors without sufficient pay or security.

How much do you think I was paid?

Did you guess? I don't even have to hear it and I can still tell you: it's lower.

But this isn't about money—except that it is about money, in the way money signals investment and importance, and what our money is invested in is meaningful.

"Teaching in Thin Air"

We know quite a bit about the conditions under which sound teaching of writing occurs.

The Conference of College Composition and Communication (CCCC), a collective that draws on the research and insights of writing teachers across the entire country and seeks to promote this wisdom, has developed a list of twelve principles for the teaching of postsecondary writing:

1. Sound writing instruction emphasizes the rhetorical nature of writing.
2. Sound writing instruction considers the needs of real audiences.
3. Sound writing instruction recognizes writing as a social act.
4. Sound writing instruction enables students to analyze and practice with a variety of genres.
5. Sound writing instruction recognizes writing processes as iterative and complex.
6. Sound writing instruction depends upon frequent, timely, and context-specific feedback to students from an experienced postsecondary instructor.
7. Sound writing instruction emphasizes relationships between writing and technologies.
8. Sound writing instruction supports learning, engagement, and critical thinking in courses across the curriculum.
9. Sound writing instruction provides students with the support necessary to achieve their goals.
10. Sound writing instruction extends from a knowledge of theories of writing (including, but not limited to, those theories developed in the field of composition and rhetoric).
11. Sound writing instruction is provided by instructors with reasonable and equitable working conditions.

12. Sound writing instruction is assessed through a collaborative effort that focuses on student learning within and beyond a writing course.[1]

If we consider what it means to write and practice writing, these principles are entirely unsurprising. We can be glad the CCCC put common sense into words, but it wasn't strictly necessary.

For the moment, I'd like to focus on principle eleven: "Sound writing instruction is provided by instructors with reasonable and equitable working conditions."

Among the criteria making up this principle are "adequate resources—including (but not limited to) time, reasonable class sizes, and physical surroundings—to provide sound writing instruction."

"Instructors should also earn a living wage and receive health coverage and other benefits."

Teaching loads should be no more than 20 students per class—with an ideal load of 15—and "no English faculty members should teach more than 60 writing students a term."

These course and student loads are important, because as Susan Schorn, a curriculum specialist for writing at the University of Texas at Austin, says,

> Teaching students to write well requires intense, individualized teacher-student interaction. Effective writing instructors read every word a student has written (including those that don't mean what the student intends them to mean), puzzling through incomplete, tangled, or overstuffed sentences. They piece together the idea the student was most likely trying to communicate, and judge how well the resulting document fulfills the goals of the assignment. Then they respond—perhaps in one-on-one meetings, perhaps in writing—describing what the student has done successfully, and how he or she might make the writing stronger, more complex, more clear.[2]

Teaching writing is a lot like coaching. There are many things you can communicate to the entire team at once, but at some point you need to work one-on-one on the specific difficulties each player is having. It is both time consuming and occasionally frustrating to say highly similar things in individual conferences, but it is also necessary.

A golf instructor watches your swing, tells you what you did wrong when you hooked it into the parking lot, breaking the back window of someone's BMW, offers an adjustment, sees you slice the next one two holes over, and keeps offering adjustments until you finally start to figure it out on your own. Whether the learning happens is ultimately on the performer, but a good instructor works at identifying and communicating the breakthrough that will allow that performer to perform.

This is teaching writing—understanding where something went wrong and helping the author set things right without ever grabbing the club and swinging at the student's ball yourself.

It has been estimated an average writing instructor takes about forty minutes per paper to do this work.[3] In my experience, this is about right, depending on the type of class, but it can also vary widely. If our job was merely to "grade" and not offer the type of feedback necessary for students to advance and improve, the time would drop to more like the three minutes spent scoring a standardized assessment, but this is not the job of teachers.

I often can predict a grade on an assignment from the opening paragraph. This skill is not rare for experienced writing teachers, but it also isn't worth much by itself.

Start multiplying the papers and the students and we begin to see the tensions between the ideal and the actual.

Schorn calls the conditions under which many college writing instructors work "teaching in thin air," like trying to exert yourself when you're at a high altitude. It's not that you can't put one foot in front of the other, but you're also constantly gasping for breath.

The air is thin for a significant number of college writing instructors, perhaps even a majority.

In fact, in my seventeen years of teaching college writing following my graduate studies, I have never experienced the CCCC's "ideal" load. Most often I have exceeded the maximum load, sometimes doubling it.

And I have been one of the lucky ones.

According to the American Association of University Professors, a majority of those teaching college are part-time employees, many of whom teach the equivalent of a full-time course load by commuting between multiple institutions.[4]

Part-timers are often referred to as "adjuncts," but an additional 17 percent of the workforce are non-tenure-track full-time faculty. In other words, over two-thirds of those teaching college are off the tenure track, without job security and often without benefits. Collectively these are called "contingent" faculty, and by every definition they are a supermajority of instructional staff.

This situation is even more pronounced in teaching first-year writing, with its heavy reliance on adjunct faculty and graduate assistants, many of whom live marginal economic existences. So-called freeway fliers do so while working at multiple institutions simultaneously, sometimes cobbling together seven or eight courses in a semester.

Some kind of "side hustle" to make ends meet is often necessary. It is not unheard of for college instructors to be homeless or even engage in sex work.[5] One study finds that one-quarter of adjunct faculty—people who have at least one post-graduate degree—rely on some form of public assistance.[6]

A significant proportion of those who are tasked to help the next generation gain the skills and experience to help them live productive and happy lives are flirting with poverty.

A Difficult Admission (Cont.)

Back to "Guess My Salary."

For those six years I worked at Clemson University, my salary was around $25,000 per year, less than the starting salary for a first grade teacher—a professional who is also tragically underpaid. The just over $3,000 per course is slightly higher than the national average for adjunct faculty. Even though I was good at my job, and even though society, at least in theory, believes the work to be important, for years I would not tell anyone my salary because I attached so much shame to that number.

I was one of the lucky non-tenure-track faculty because I held a full-time "lecturer" position, which included health insurance benefits. My partner always had a stable, well-paying job and could have supported us by herself. I earned outside income writing and editing. Because of these factors, unlike many other contingent faculty I did not experience a precarious financial existence.

I share this information not so readers will feel sorry for me. I love teaching. I was fortunate to be able to do the work I love even though I wasn't paid a professional wage. Nevertheless, the experience showed me the disconnect between the importance we claim for education in general (and teaching writing in particular) and the limited resources we dedicate to that work.

Discussing the economic, political, and social factors that have resulted in an "adjunctified" teaching workforce is beyond the scope of this book, but regardless of the causes, what is most important are the conditions on the ground, and they are not conducive to effective teaching.

Despite lip service regarding the importance of writing, institutional indifference to the conditions of writing teachers is commonplace. When the budget-crunch shit starts to flow downhill, contingent faculty, lacking any institutional power or status, are waiting at the bottom. Unfortunately, students are often standing nearby when this happens.

What happened at Arizona State University in 2014–2015 is illustrative. Stuck between a rock (increasing enrollment made necessary by declining state investment) and a hard place (the expense of hiring more faculty), ASU administration unilaterally declared they would increase the teaching load for non-tenured writing instructors from four to five courses per semester. Salaries would remain constant at $32,000 per year.[7] This would make for student loads exceeding 150 in some cases, two and a half times the recommended *maximum*.

When I wrote critically of Arizona State positioning itself as the "New American University" (a branding pushed by ASU president Michael Crow) through a series of corporate partnerships and an embrace of algorithmic teaching, even as the instructor loads were being increased, Mark Johnson, senior director for Media Relations and Strategic Communications, whose salary was equivalent to just under that of five instructors added together,[8] replied in a comment, "While recommended class loads fit the ideals of academic associations, they are a luxury ill-afforded by a university trying to educate a growing population and workforce of tomorrow."

Recommended maximum student loads as determined by disciplinary experts should not be viewed as a "luxury." I do not intend to pick on ASU specifically, because their treatment of contingent faculty is quite typical for institutions of their kind. But what happened at ASU illustrates the tensions within a system that prevents the resourcing of teaching writing and the ways administrations respond to those tensions.

Doing things right is called a "luxury," but there are certainly institutions with these luxuries: elite private institutions such as those making up the Ivy League, or small liberal arts colleges that prioritize instruction. The vast majority of undergraduate students, however, have at least some instructors who are working in thin air. This is most true for the least advantaged and least prepared students at non-selective four-year institutions and community colleges where the resources are stretched thinnest.

Even though these conditions are often poor, good teaching still happens. I am proud of much of the work I've done in the classroom, but I am well acquainted with the inevitable compromises made necessary by having too many students and too few resources. Twenty-minute conferences shrink to fifteen and then ten minutes. Seven major writing assignments become six and then five because every time I would collect an assignment it meant setting aside most waking hours in a weekend so I might return it to students on a timely basis, while protecting my weekday time to meet writing obligations necessary to bring in additional income.

Other contingent faculty I've worked with over the years have driven for Uber, waited tables, babysat, tutored, pulled weekend shifts at Jiffy Lube, or taught three sections at the local community college simultaneously with their "full-time" teaching at our home institution. All honorable work, but a pace that is unsustainable and not conducive to effective teaching. There is no time for professional development. There is barely enough time for adequate rest.

In the 2016–2017 academic year, when I had stepped down to a single course each semester, I was paid $2650 per course, $11 an hour by my calculation.

If writing matters, we must resource the teaching of writing.

In this sense, the fate of the contingent writing instructor looks like that of a lot of other workers in America, where greater and greater productivity is squeezed out of us without seeing any individual gains.

We cannot divorce the conditions under which people are required to work from the work itself. Those conditions must include the physical and emotional well-being of teachers as well as students.

A Vow of Poverty: Life as a K–12 Teacher

The greatest trick the devil ever pulled was convincing a significant proportion of Americans that teachers were overpaid and had too much security. In reality, particularly compared to the practices in other developed countries, our K–12 teachers are considerably overworked and underpaid.

All of the conditions conspiring to make school atmospheres inhospitable to student learning also make for difficult teaching atmospheres for instructors. In some ways, it is worse for instructors. Students (for the most part) aren't at risk of being fired.

Teachers in the United States spend 38 percent more time in the classroom than those in other developed countries.[9]

Almost half of teachers say they experience "a lot" of daily stress. As compared with other professions, teachers are "least likely to report feeling like their 'opinions seem to count.'"[10]

As Daniel Koretz of Harvard shows in *The Testing Charade*, public school teachers have been subjected to year after year of shifting external demands for accountability, each change more oppressive and draconian than the last. School reform has resulted in testing regimes that have "sometimes been taken to lengths that are both absurd and cruel." For example, after Florida introduced Value Added Modeling (VAM) for teacher evaluation, an eleventh and twelfth grade math teacher with thirty years of experience found that 50 percent of her performance evaluation was based on the performance on a reading test of tenth grade students she had never taught.[11]

A 2015 survey of thirty thousand teachers found their greatest source of stress was "having to carry out a stream of new initiatives—such as implementing curricula and testing related to the Common Core State Standards—without being given adequate training."[12]

This combination of overwork, lack of agency, and what often feels like arbitrary assessment results in high rates of teacher burnout, which in turn leads to teacher turnover, teachers either switching schools or leaving the profession altogether. Sixteen percent of teachers per year are either quitting or switching schools, most commonly due to "dissatisfaction," with over half citing it as an "important" reason for leaving. This dissatisfaction primarily stems from frustration over assessments and accountability.[13]

The negative effects of turnover are obvious. Schools absorb replacement costs as they must continually bring in new staff. Student achievement tends to be lower in schools with high turnover, and given that we know good work environments allow for better teaching and professional development, the opportunities for schools to work with a stable cadre of dedicated, mutually supportive professionals are choked off.

All of this trickles down to students who do not have the benefit of experienced, unstressed teachers who are given sufficient time and resources to develop their teaching practices. I cannot imagine another profession where we would expect professionals to tolerate the kind of interference that is routine in the lives of primary and secondary education teachers.

I have taught only at the college level—I don't have the gumption to handle a K–12 classroom—but I can testify that teaching is enormously difficult, and it takes many years to build an expertise. There is no substitute for experience in this pursuit. Teaching, like writing, is an extended exercise in failure. You make a plan, do your best to execute, have some portion of your ass handed to you by circumstances and events you could not foresee, and try to do better next time around.

This makes teaching challenging, but for people who are called to it, teaching offers fulfillment that is hard to match. Unfortunately, because teaching is a calling for many, teachers are ripe for exploitation. I tell students, "my condolences" when I find out they are education majors, and they smile ruefully, understanding.

More and more, teaching has become a kind of priesthood, where its entrants know they are consigned to a vow of poverty upon entry. A report from the Economic Policy Institute found that teachers make 17 percent less than workers with comparable experience and education. The gap was less than 2 percent just over twenty years ago.[14]

The increasing cost of college combined with an employment structure requiring the pursuit of additional degrees for career advancement has created a generation of new teachers saddled with intractable debt. In an NPR survey on student debt among teachers, 52 percent of respondents rated their concern over their student debt as a four or five on a five-point scale, where five equals "terrified."[15]

Respondents said things like:

"I feel like I'll be making the last payment from my grave."

"I am overloaded and struggling. It's terrifying."

"It is an albatross around my neck. Years of paying and I feel like I'm getting nowhere."

For all the importance we claim for education and teaching writing, there is little evidence that we resource it as something important. If we want good teaching of writing to happen we need to put teachers in a position to be good at their jobs while incentivizing continual training and renewal of their own practices.

Instead, we grind them down until they are forced out of the profession. I have seen dozens of qualified, dedicated college instructors who have no desire to quit teaching leave because they could no longer countenance doing such important work for so little money.

I count myself among them.

And remember, I was one of the lucky ones.

PART THREE

A New Framework

Why School?

....

What's It All For?

Over time, we have erected a system that is punishing to students, exploitive of teachers, and largely divorced from what we know about how and why students learn. It needs remaking.

The remaking of our entire system of education would take several more books to explore, but I would like to illustrate how we can return to the values most of us already share through the lens of how we teach writing. Doing this requires starting with some fundamental questions.

Why school? What is the purpose of school? What should happen in school?

We can perhaps agree that the purpose of school is to enhance the intellectual, social, and emotional capacities of students. Schools should be places oriented toward learning and growth, potentials explored and fulfilled. Yes, we hope that school prepares students for higher education and/or jobs and careers, but can we agree that enhancing the intellectual, social, and emotional capacities of students is likely to lead to these outcomes?

To achieve desirable outcomes, I believe those capacities should take the form of what Ken Bain, education researcher and author of *What the Best College Students Do*, calls "deep learning," essentially learning that can be adapted to new and unfamiliar challenges.[1]

In other words, deep learning allows students to extend something they've encountered in one situation to another situation, even when those situations may not seem obviously related. Students who are subject to deep learning show significantly better outcomes both in school and life beyond school. Students are educated, rather than trained. Furthermore, as shown in the research of Bain and others, including the Gallup-Purdue Index Report, students who experience deep learning are also more likely to go on to have successful and fulfilling careers.

Learning will take care of helping to make sure students lead "productive" lives, particularly if we allow students to determine what "productive" means for themselves.

This is an obviously idealized notion, and many conditions and circumstances conspire to keep us from achieving the ideal; but agreeing on an underlying set of goals and values seems important.

Not everyone will agree. I have conversations with some who prefer to think of school as a proving ground, a test where the worthy triumph and the wanting wither.

Those who share this view have the benefit of knowing that school already essentially reflects these values. We call it a meritocracy while failing to recognize the different starting lines afforded those who won the birth lottery—but perhaps one's parents and social capital are properly viewed as part of one's "merit." However, having been born with many of these advantages, I disagree. I have endeavored to become as successful a person as I am able, and yet I am quite certain that if I hadn't had the advantage of being born to two successful college graduates (who were also children of college graduates), and raised in a wealthy Chicago suburb, you would not be reading these words.

I believe in the virtues of hard work and diligence as much as anybody, but I've probably required less than average portions of each to get where I am today. This doesn't cause me a moment of shame or guilt, but it would be wrong not to recognize reality.

If you believe school is properly viewed as something like ancient Sparta, where warriors earn the spoils while the rest can pound sand, much of what I have to say on this subject will sound like the rantings of a soft-hearted dreamer entirely divorced from the "real world."

Maybe so, and there was a time when I would have agreed with some of those critiques, but I've come to see school in general, and our approach to teaching writing in particular, as diametrically opposed to fulfilling the goals we claim for education.

Regardless of one's educational philosophies, there is broad agreement that students don't learn as much or as well as they should. Cultural faith in the meritocracy seems to be holding, but in truth we have students busy competing in games that are significantly rigged for trophies already etched with other people's names.

As we've seen with the steadily increasing rates of depression and anxiety among students, even the "winners" of our education competitions are more accurately described as "casualties."

To think we can raise every student's "achievement" as defined by our current system of schooling and we will somehow fulfill the promise of enhancing the intellectual, social, and emotional capacities of students is magical thinking.

There is no curricular or pedagogical intervention by itself that will fix what ails schools.

In fact, it's best if we stop thinking about schools ailing or failing or otherwise being "broken." The narrative of school failure has allowed for "reforms" more likely to impose additional burdens on those who already work under the greatest disadvantages. The failing-schools narrative causes us to lurch from fad to fad in an effort to turn the ship around. Trying to fix schools while not paying sufficient attention to the people who populate those schools has only led to a system increasingly antithetical to learning, and even toxic to students' mental and physical well-being.

Curriculum Isn't Going to Save Us

Addressing the underlying conditions of poverty and inequality directly will have a far more beneficial effect, far more quickly than any curriculum could ever hope to achieve.

While there are a whole host of interventions we could undertake to help students better learn, the most immediate, straightforward, and cost-effective route to improving student achievement in school is to make sure every child has access to appropriate nutrition and arrives in school having had sufficient rest.

Thirteen million children experience food insecurity—lack of access to nutritious food on a regular basis—and programs such as free lunch and breakfast only partially close these gaps.[2] Hungry students are less likely to retain information, they have a more difficult time regulating their moods, they can't concentrate, and they are more likely to experience stress.

Food insecurity and homelessness does not disappear when students enter college. Twenty-two percent of college students experience "very low levels of food security" according to a 2016 report from the National Student Campaign against Hunger and Homelessness.[3] Those same students have an increased likelihood of homelessness. As reported in a paper from Sara Goldrick-Rab and Katharine Broton, sociologists who study systemic barriers preventing students from achieving their higher education goals, over half of students who report experiencing homelessness were working at least thirty hours per week.[4] It is hard to consider education a meritocracy when you can be working essentially full-time while still going to school and experiencing homelessness.

If students cannot afford food and shelter, they are unlikely to be able to pay for textbooks or other school-related resources we now view as necessary for success, such as computers.

If students are not properly fueled, they cannot learn. If they are tired, they cannot think.

Dr. Wendy Troxel, a behavioral scientist and expert in sleep research, calls sleep deprivation among American teenagers "an epidemic," with only one in ten getting the eight to ten hours of recommended sleep per night. Teenage brains are in a hyper-speed period of brain development, forming the very capacities we claim to be most important for learning—critical reasoning, problem solving, good judgment—and for those brains to grow healthy, teenagers need sleep. School days cannot start at 7 a.m. Homework should not gobble up hours upon hours of post-school time. Activities pursued in the name of boosting college applications need to be weighed against the cost of sleep deprivation and the resulting stress, anxiety, and depression.

In Dr. Troxel's research on thirty thousand students, for each hour of lost sleep, "there was a 38 percent increase in feeling sad or hopeless, and a 58 percent increase in teen suicide attempts."[5]

Unless we establish a baseline where students are physically, mentally, and emotionally fueled for learning, all the ideas I'm about to share that will transform how we go about teaching writing will fail to have maximum impact.

We must recognize that our current schooling systems operate under particular ideologies and those ideologies should be up for questioning. When someone claims they want to "increase student achievement," we should be asking, Increase how? Achieving what? These are not value-neutral propositions. Different values and ideologies will point toward different solutions. If you believe contemporary America is, and properly should be, analogous to ancient Sparta, we probably owe it to students to train them to be Spartans.

But I believe those values are inconsistent with the American ideal of life, liberty, and the pursuit of happiness. To pursue that ideal means rethinking our ideologies, starting with our views of students.

As for writing instruction, the first step down the road of progress is to spend much less time worrying about the writing as demonstrated through largely meaningless assessments and instead pay intention to the writers themselves.

Reality Pedagogy

Dr. Christopher Emdin, associate professor of math, science, and technology at Teachers College, Columbia University, had a rough first year in his previous career as a secondary school teacher at an urban school.

Despite having been raised in a neighborhood like the one he was teaching in, he found himself "nervous" on his first day as he anticipated facing the students.

The categorizing of which students were "teachable" or the opposite ("good" or "bad") became "a game of sorts" for Emdin and the other teachers. He was counseled not to express too much emotion lest he appear vulnerable and to "stand your ground when they test you."

"Don't smile until November" became the teachers' mantra. School was a battleground between teachers and students; the teacher's job was to civilize the savages.

Emdin was uneasy with this approach from the beginning: "The teachers' venting sessions reminded me of my experiences in high school and how I was forced to obey rules without an opportunity to question whether they supported the way I learned. As a high school student, the more I engaged in school, the more I learned about the rules that guided the institution and realized they ran counter to the ways I experienced the world."[6]

Reflecting on his life as a student and his work as a teacher, Emdin realized, "I had been trained my entire life to believe that becoming something other than who I truly was would make me a better person."

While a pedagogy focused on student defects is not unique to inner-city schools, in those communities it is particularly corrosive. Emdin began to see the school as a mechanism by which "all the fight was squeezed out" of students. The overwhelming ethos was one of control and compliance, and in the case of the black and brown students at the school where Emdin worked, this required them to sacrifice their own cultures in order to conform to a largely unexamined "ideal." As a student, Emdin found it disorienting and alienating. As a teacher, after a period of adjustment, he vowed to do something about it.

In response, Emdin has developed a practice he calls "reality pedagogy"—"an approach to teaching and learning that has a primary goal of meeting each student on his or her own cultural and emotional turf. It focuses on making the local experiences of the student visible and creating contexts where there is a role reversal of sorts that positions the student as the expert in his or her own teaching and learning, and the teacher is the learner."[7]

Emdin's "reality pedagogy" makes use of structures and techniques that involve the students themselves in shaping and defining the community in which they will be learning. As one example, Emdin employs the "cogenerative dialogue" or "cogens," "simple conversations between the teacher and their students with a goal of co-generating/generating plans of action for improving the classroom."[8]

Emdin's approach recognizes that student learners possess valid knowledge about how they best learn and are capable of being fully collaborative inside a classroom community.

As we've seen, our current system of schooling, built on standardization, compliance, and surveillance, is not only ineffective in helping students learn; it is actively damaging to their physical and mental well-being. They are subjected to a culture that systematically devalues and degrades their individuality. Emdin challenges this framework, demanding that students take charge of their own learning by clearly identifying their own goals and articulating the best routes to those goals. It is a far more demanding and rigorous approach than a curriculum that demands compliance with teacher authority above all.

The alienating nature of school is experienced not only by students at the urban secondary schools in which Christopher Emdin taught. I've seen the same effect in the diverse array of college students coming from many different backgrounds I've worked with at four different institutions over the last seventeen years.[9] The ways we erase their cultures and desires may differ, but the end result is similar.

"I Can't Wait Until I Retire"

I will never forget the college sophomore who sighed deeply and declared she could not wait until she could retire.

We were in a class discussion about the novel *Everything Matters!* by Ron Currie Jr. The novel centers on Junior Thibodeau, who is "gifted" with the knowledge that the world will end when he is thirty-six years and 168 days old, when a comet slams into planet Earth.

Burdened with this knowledge, Junior must live his life. It is a wonderful book with a lunatic (in the best way) plot, and you can imagine how knowing such a thing could mess you up. The narrative asks us to contemplate what truly "matters" in life, and in preparation for our discussion of the novel, I put a slide on the screen at the front of the room with these three prompts:

- List five things you can't live without.
- List five things you want to do in your life and why you want to do them.
- List five things you want your partner in life to be (if you want a partner).

And I asked these three questions:

- How did what matters to you come to matter to you? (What are the roots of what you value?)

- How do we measure if a life "matters?"
- How will you know if your life "matters?"

While I did intend to put students in a contemplative place, I did not think I'd be triggering any kind of existential crisis. I asked students to sketch out answers in their notes and in a few minutes we would discuss them as a class.

Over the years, I have become increasingly careful about the kind of language and wording I use in class to signal the purpose of our activities. At one time, I would have said something like "What did you write down?" but by this point, I had switched to "What did you learn?"

The sophomore's hand shot up. Raising hands wasn't strictly necessary, as class tended to be a little more free-flowing, but I nodded and she said, "I learned I can't wait until I retire."

"Why's that?" I said.

"Because that's when I'll finally get to do everything I want to do."

Her list of five things she wanted to do included career goals ("making a difference") and a desire for world travel, and she recognized (correctly) the things she wanted to do would be both time consuming and costly (in terms of both money and forgoing other opportunities). The other major desire on her list was "get married and have children."

In her view, her desire to see the world could not be reconciled with the time and monetary demands of raising a family while simultaneously building a career that would allow her family sufficient material comfort and meet her goal of "making a difference." These other deep desires would have to wait for some indefinite future.

I wish I had come up with what happened next, but the interests of truth and accuracy require me to report that it was another student who had this insight. This other student said, "She said, 'I can't wait until I retire,' which means she has to wait to do everything she wants to do, but 'I can't wait until I retire' means, like, *don't* wait until you retire to do what you want to do."

Out of the mouths of babes . . .

This first student, no more than nineteen years old, had adopted an ethos where every moment of her life, particularly her school life, was designed as preparation for some future moment, and presumably, at some point all of this furious work would pay off, that point being—in this particular student's mind—retirement, a date forty-five or fifty years in the future.

During the discussion, the class explored the tension between two interpretations of "I can't wait until I retire," in the context of a novel where the main character knows the exact date the world will end. On the one hand, they recognized putting off the pursuit of their desires carried a significant risk. *I could be hit by a bus on the way home from class.*

Or a meteorite could strike Earth, ending civilization.

On the other hand, for many, the risk of deviating from the necessary pathway to financial prosperity seemed awfully risky. Life was like a race with no real finish line. High school begat college, begat more school or career, begat career advancement, and so on, until . . . retirement, when a life focused on one's desires could finally be realized.

The popular image of college students partying because college is a time without care is out of date. It's more likely students are seeking anesthesia against a world filled with worries.

Somewhere along the line we collectively decided, without actually agreeing, that school is primarily about preparing the future workers of America for their jobs.

Maybe it's rooted in the Reagan Administration's *A Nation at Risk*. According to that report our country's greatness was rooted not in values like freedom, life, and liberty, but our ability to beat the Japanese on standardized tests. Thirty-five years later we have arrived at a place where the kindergarten pageant must be canceled to help make students "college- and career-ready."[10]

High school teacher Peter Greene has tracked examples of the mindset that "education's main or sole aim is to prepare children to be the worker bees of tomorrow, to become a 'product' to be consumed by the future corporate overlords."[11] These are some of his examples:

> Allan Golston of the Gates Foundation: "Businesses are the primary consumers of the output of our schools."

> Rex Tillerson when he was CEO of Exxon: "I'm not sure public schools understand that we're their customer—that we, the business community, are your customer. What they don't understand is they are producing a product at the end of that high school graduation."

> The Florida state legislature: "The purpose of the public education system of Florida is to develop the intellect of the citizens, to contribute to the economy, to create an effective workforce, and to prepare students for a job."

Taken together, these sentiments suggest the purpose of school is to shape students into something suitable for consumption by corporations. Students being individuals with different backgrounds or hopes or dreams is immaterial. It is a vision of American values that substitutes gainful employment for freedom. In Greene's words:

> This is all alarming because it is such a narrow, cramped, tiny vision of education, a low bar to clear, an unworthy target at which to aim. All the depth and breadth of human experience, all the joy and heartfelt fulfillment to which humans can aspire, all the glorious discovery of one's best self, all the varied and beautiful experience of being a human in the world—these folks would have us toss all of that away to better turn children into meat widgets who can serve not their own human aspirations and dreams and goals, but the corporate need for drones to fill jobs so that the rich can get richer.

I couldn't say it better myself. I do not deny that we should hope our children grow up one day to be productive adults, but children are not properly viewed as future products for business; they are human beings, small ones who are still learning and figuring stuff out.

And college students are adults who should be encouraged to practice their own agency in the pursuit of their desires, rather than feeling yoked to a treadmill whose speed increases with each successive year.

Life is to be lived, including the years between five and twenty-two years old. A world that suggests those years are merely preparation for the real stuff, and the real stuff is almost entirely defined by your college and/or career, is an awfully impoverished place. Fat, drunk, and stupid is no way to go through life, but neither is sleepless, stressed, and medicated.

It's also a bad way to get students interested in learning, which is supposedly our goal.

Learning Is Life; Life Is Learning

In "My Pedagogic Creed" from 1897, John Dewey declared, "I believe that education, therefore, is a process of living, and not a preparation for future living."[12] Our current system, which posits school as training for college and career, fails on two fronts. It's poor preparation for the kinds of learning students are expected to do in college and life, and it denies them the full experience of life during those school years.

Writing is a skill, but it is a skill that lives inside the person and that often develops through idiosyncratic and individually driven processes. The best ways to demonstrate that skill may vary from occasion to occasion and person to person. We want writers to understand what's appropriate in a given rhetorical situation, but we also should value writers who are able to express some aspect of themselves inside those situations.

We should also operate under the assumption that every student needs to prepare for the long haul of life as a writer because in truth, these days, everyone is a writer. With text messaging, with the proliferation of social media platforms, with whatever else some Silicon Valley madperson (I mean genius) is dreaming up next, it's likely each successive generation of students will do much more writing and text-based communication than the previous one.

Consider Slack, which serves as a kind of background communication tool amalgamating email, texting, and a closed Twitter reserved for a particular set of employees. Even for people whose jobs require little formal writing, they will be expected to consistently communicate through these media, and that communication will be fraught with peril if they are not attentive to audience and purpose.

In the 2016 election and its aftermath we have seen Facebook and Twitter become weaponized town squares where citizens of different perspectives do verbal battle, joined in and stoked by armies of bots purposefully sowing distrust and misinformation. Stanford research suggests that students (and just about everyone else) are poor at "reasoning about information," frequently failing to discern outright fakes from legitimate sources.[13]

This reality is part of the new literacy in which students must live and work, and education is obligated to help prepare students for it. Cathy Davidson, co-founder and director of HASTAC, a collaboration focused on educational innovation, argues that English departments (and the humanities in general) must act as "society's keeper of two of the three R's of traditional literacy, namely, 'reading' and 'writing.'"[14]

But these literacies are not fixed in stone. The library skills needed to use the *Reader's Guide to Periodical Literature* and the card catalog are irrelevant in a world of databases at our fingertips. And yet, students are often required to work with information in ways that more resemble what I did in grade school almost forty years ago than in ways that reflect our interconnected world.

The ability to critically consume and produce text will be a near-universal need in the United States going forward. One could argue we've already reached a crisis point on this front. To do better means introducing lessons in Internet literacy that extend well beyond traditional approaches to teaching and learning in academic contexts. Writing instruction will need to be the front line in helping students figure out what is shit and what is shinola.

Schools therefore will need to adapt, moving away from an approach that focuses on "academics" and instead taking a broader view when it comes to helping individuals develop as writers and thinkers. Academic writing is a genre like any other. We should not pretend it is the only context in which one can learn to communicate effectively. We can determine what kinds of thinking and reasoning academic study requires and have students practice those ways of thinking with significantly greater depth and in many different ways.

There is no direct route to learning to write. We should be giving students a range of experiences so they can build an array of tools and approaches to turn to for any given writing situation. We must stop asking student writers to adopt a kind of generic "scholar" persona simply to perform competency and pretend erudition, and instead give them the necessary room to develop their own beliefs about the world around them.

I am tempted to say that the way to improve student writing is to simply do the opposite of everything we've been doing. In a way, this is true. It would be difficult to design a system more poorly suited to our putative goals than the one we have.

Setting things on a better path *is* fairly straightforward: we need to change the things we value and bring them into alignment with what we know works for creating situations conducive to learning in general and learning to write in particular.

These should be our goals:

1. We seek to increase educational challenges while simultaneously decreasing student stress and anxiety related to writing.
2. We seek to change the orientation of school from only preparing students (poorly, as it turns out) for the indefinite future to also living and learning in the present.
3. We seek to provide experiences designed around learning and growth, rather than giving assignments and testing for competencies.
4. We will end the tyranny of grades and replace them with self-assessment and reflection.
5. We will give teachers sufficient time, freedom, and resources to teach effectively. In return, they will be required to embrace the same ethos of self-assessment and reflection expected of students.

These goals are ambitious, and they will require coordination among many different people with many different roles in our educational systems, but all of them are eminently doable. But achieving them requires challenging the ideologies that have dominated education and guided (so-called) education reform for going on thirty-plus years.

Increasing Rigor

Current common approaches for teaching writing are simultaneously too punishing and not nearly challenging enough.

Part of the problem is how "rigor" is viewed in education. "Rigor" means "strictness" and "severity." It is an artifact of a different time and a different mentality toward schooling. It remains popular mostly as a way to invoke days of yore that are supposedly better than today.

Back in my day blah blah blah. Snow blah blah blah. And we liked it blah blah blah.

But when students say a class was "hard," they often mean "confusing" or "arbitrary," rather than stimulating and challenging.

This particular flavor of educational rigor exists as a form of educational folklore, and if learning is our goal, it is bad framing. A body in rigor experiences a sudden cold sensation coupled with profuse sweating, like in a fever. Rigor mortis is stiff and dead. Neither of these should be used to describe learning.

We should seek to make education as challenging as we can manage, but that challenge shouldn't invoke images of punishment or, in the case of rigor, actual death. As we've seen, students do very little writing, and the writing they do is often in the service of proving competency on standardized assessments. Today's students do not suffer from a deficiency in writing skill—remember: they make about the same number of errors as previous generations—but instead have experienced a deeply impoverished notion of what writing does and how it works.

Rather than exploring the different kinds of thinking and doing writers engage with in their work, students tend to repeat the same activities, over and over again, which is how we wind up in a place where all roads end at the five-paragraph essay.

In reality, students have not been practicing the "basics," and because of this, they haven't been sufficiently challenged by writing.

The True Basics of Writing

In grade school, we were required to try our hand at playing an instrument. Along with about thirty of my fellow fourth graders, I wanted the drums.[1]

I ended up with the clarinet. I did not want to play the clarinet, even when my teacher told us Benny Goodman, the greatest musician/composer/arranger of all time, had played the clarinet. Sax, okay. Trumpet, if I have to. Clarinet? Can I try out for the drums again?

Absent choice, I accepted my clarinet and began weekly in-school lessons (a different era, for sure). Unlike with a saxophone or a trumpet, it is easy to make sound with the clarinet out of the gate. Unfortunately, it is much easier to make a "goose in its final death throes" sound with a clarinet than it is to make a clarinet sound with the clarinet. Basically, put your mouth over the end and blow, and voilà! Mortally wounded waterfowl.

To make a clarinet sound with a clarinet, you must be able to make a clarinet "embouchure," which involves a combination of proper lip and tooth position and breath control, something I could not do successfully even by the third lesson while others had essentially gotten it the first day.

To play the clarinet, you need the basic skill of the embouchure. Without it, no clarinet playing.

If writing is also a skill, and I believe it to be, it's worth asking: What is its foundational unit?

Some believe that it is the sentence, and if we want to teach students to write, we need to first work on the "basics" of the sentence.

This may make intuitive sense, but those people are wrong.

I understand the allure of first focusing on the sentence. Teaching sentences is straightforward, explicable, and when you drill sentences (as I have done), you fairly quickly see a kind of progress, as all those "correct" (or correct-ish) sentences begin to look something like writing. Perhaps this really is the equivalent of the clarinetist's embouchure. We may not be making music, exactly, but at least that terrible honking noise has stopped.

And of course, this approach is validated by standardized tests that favor surface-level "correctness" over depth of ideas. It's a good strategy to help students make things that at least resemble writing, which is pleasing indeed when they were previously making things that did not even resemble writing.

Nevertheless, the sentence is not the basic skill or fundamental unit of writing.

The idea is.

In fact, as almost everyone has experienced as they write, the final specifics of the sentence are often the very last thing to take shape in a piece of writing. When experienced writers struggle over sentences the battle is not about "correctness," as we teach developing writers, but in lassoing the words that best express the idea. Even for experienced writers, perhaps especially for experienced writers, the earliest sentence-making attempts in a draft are often provisional and unsatisfactory.

My own drafts are riddled with this reality, half-formed ideas expressed in half-formed sentences with notations such as: SOMETHING LIKE THIS, BUT NOT SAYING IT SO DUMB. GET IT TOGETHER IDIOT!

Telling students "First you must know your sentences and only then can you start to write" gets writing backward. When we have an idea worth expressing, the desire to share it provides the necessary intrinsic motivation to find the precise language to do so. Sentences matter very much, but they are not first.

Yes, students early on struggle with making sentences, but every writer, regardless of their level, struggles with making sentences. In fact, as teacher and writing researcher Mina Shaughnessy reports in her classic of writing studies, *Errors and Expectations*, when even experienced writers shift to an unfamiliar genre, their sentence error rate goes up. It is as though the skill of sentence writing disappears when writers are forced to work with less familiar ideas and forms.[2]

By making sentence mastery a prerequisite to actually getting to the best part of writing—the ideas—we are withholding the most pleasurable and motivating part of the act itself.

Writing is thinking, and I have yet to meet a writer who thinks in sentences. To suggest we must know sentences before we start to write is a lie.

Playing the clarinet and writing are both skills, but the analogy has limits. Unlike learning an instrument, where replication can be (but need not be) a bridge to the more sophisticated work of composition, writers of every age and experience are composing from their earliest attempts.

As it turns out, writers aren't practicing at something that's equivalent to merely playing the clarinet. Even from the start, they're practicing at being Benny Goodman, musician/composer/arranger. Of course, most of us won't become the writing equivalent of Benny Goodman, but if we're not making the attempt and engaging with writing in all of its messy, confounding dimensions, it's hard to argue we're truly writing at all.

As I consider the attitudes students bring to the college writing classroom, I realize that in a school context, no matter how many words they may have generated prior to college, very few of them have been asked to write. They have been trained to pass those writing-related assessments.

To get students writing, we have to put them to work making meaning.

Making Writing Meaningful by Making Meaningful Writing

....

A Chef's Life

If we want students to write well and develop the attitudes, skills, knowledge, and habits of mind of the writing practice, it follows that we should create the conditions under which they can do their best work.

But before thinking about writing, I want to consider the question in general: Under what conditions do you do your *best* work?

To illustrate, let's go back to a chef. To do their best work a chef needs:

1. Access to good, fresh ingredients, including enough to repeat a dish if it comes out wrong
2. Access to all necessary equipment for food preparation and cooking
3. Appropriate help from others—such as line cooks
4. Sufficient time to plan the meal prior to cooking
5. Sufficient time to execute the meal while cooking
6. Diners who are anticipating the meal

I believe we can put these conditions into three categories: resources, time, and motivation. Items 1–3 deal with resources, items 4 and 5 cover time, and item 6 is motivation.

Almost regardless of one's field, doing good work requires some combination of sufficient resources, time, and motivation. The specifics may change, but the principles remain. My guess is the list for your own field looks pretty similar to what chefs need.

This principle even extends beyond professional work. The same frame can apply to parenting or being a good partner.

When we have enough time, resources, and motivation, success isn't guaranteed, but its likelihood increases significantly.

Writing is similar to being a chef. With writing, I need sufficient resources, time, and motivation to do my best work.

I do my best work when:

1. I am passionate about my subject and have the freedom to write about my interests.
2. I am knowledgeable (enough) about my subject.
3. I can easily access research or information I don't possess that may inform what I am writing.
4. I have sufficient (but not too much) time to engage in a writing process appropriate to the occasion.
5. I am sufficiently rested and mentally alert.
6. I have an audience potentially interested in reading my writing.
7. I have a deep understanding of the purpose of what I am writing, why I am writing it, and what effect I hope to have on the audience.
8. I am likely to learn something via the act of writing that I did not previously know.
9. I am backstopped by trustworthy colleagues who edit and review my work with an eye toward enhancing the message and purpose of my writing.

We can easily divide my list into the categories of resources, time, and motivation.

Resources

My resource needs are relatively limited, and yet without them, I'm lost. I write exclusively on a computer or other word processor where I can type. My handwriting is insufficiently speedy or accurate to keep up with my brain, and my tendency to revise as I go also makes handwriting infeasible.

I see my existing knowledge base as a resource, though it also bleeds into motivation. What I know and believe about what I'm writing has a significant impact on the quality of the outcome. I am fortunate to have considerable freedom to write inside my own field of expertise, so I occasionally forget how important this is, but when I'm tasked with writing outside my expertise, I am reminded how vital a resource knowledge can be.

Because I don't know everything and often forget things I'm supposed to know, Internet access for research or reflection purposes is vital. Cutting me off from outside information or inspiration will shut down the work pretty quickly. Thoreau could go to Walden and hang out in a cabin and think big thoughts. Not me.

Without at least a virtual connection to the world you'd find me in that cabin making motorboat sounds with my lips.

Rest and energy are vital for me to do good work. They are a necessary resource, since I find writing very taxing, and anything that fogs my thoughts keeps me from producing.

Editorial backup usually comes very late in my own process, but knowing it is coming is vital to my own productivity and performance. It allows me to drive forward with my ideas, knowing that if they don't jell, someone will be on hand to help me fix them. While I strive to provide clean copy, I don't have to worry too much about the finest points of grammar because I have a safety net to keep from embarrassing myself.

Time

Like most people, particularly when it comes to writing, I am a procrastinator. (About 80 percent or more of my students say they procrastinate on their writing assignments.) I procrastinate not out of hating writing but out of a fear of not being able to pull off what I'm trying to do (another phenomenon that is often manifested in my students). My confidence waxes and wanes, particularly when I'm engaged in a longer project. I have met writers who do not struggle with impostor syndrome, but they are relatively rare. Perhaps they also do not struggle with procrastination.

With practice, I have learned that the only way to overcome this fear is to just start writing. Once I'm engaged with the moment-to-moment struggles, I forget to be afraid. I've often found some measure of deadline pressure useful in honing my focus. On the other hand, too much pressure, or an unexpected shift in deadlines, will knock me into paralysis. It's a fine line.

Motivation

Half of my list deals with motivation. And importantly, for me, almost all of the motivation is intrinsic/internal, as opposed to extrinsic/external.

My mother, my biggest supporter, also has long wondered why I can't write the kind of book lots of people want to read, like *The Da Vinci Code* or *Twilight*. I have wondered this myself, because I am a fan of money and the things one can buy with it.

I have even tried writing commercial fiction. Following the publication of my novel, which featured an unlikable protagonist in the midst of a crisis, I tried to write a book with characters people would like and root for. I made it through about fifty thousand words before I began to loathe the characters because I was trying so hard to make them likable. When I write fiction, I seem attracted almost exclusively to characters I want to punish on the way to partial redemption. Even this book would have more commercial potential if I were willing to position it as a panacea, and admit less complexity as to what ails the state of writing instruction.

Yes, I write for money, and seeing my name on a book provides a brief thrill, but the thrill is not what gets me to the computer.

I write about writing and teaching writing because I think there is no more important skill for students to learn. On the first day of class I tell students that writing is a pathway to being a better and more contented human being. I tell them writing will make them capable of experiencing empathy for others while also acting with personal agency inside a complex and contradictory world.

I believe that.

I believe that because writing is a route toward the joy of discovery, of using writing as a tool to understand myself and the world. I am at my best when during the process I am surprised by what shows up on the page.

It is akin to the "runner's high," the feeling you are somehow better than you could have believed.

Those moments do not happen every day. Sometimes they don't happen for a couple weeks or more. But the memory of when it does happen is enough to sustain me through the down times.

Writing is a highly challenging, endlessly frustrating pursuit that delivers lasting pleasure and knowledge. This aspect of writing should not be reserved for professional writers. It should be available to anyone who must write for any occasion.

As we have seen, students rarely have access to the conditions and experiences that will allow them to do their best work. Their motivation is generally limited to getting good grades, which we know to be inferior to intrinsic motivation. They often are not given the agency that allows them to write about subjects of interest.

And most of the "support" they are given comes in the form of judgment, which tends to focus on their defects, rather than their virtues, or if not their virtues, their potential. If I received the volume of negative feedback the average student gets on their writing in school, I would give it up.

Given the conditions under which students are asked to write, we cannot expect them to embrace the challenges of writing and produce work that is not only academically accomplished, but most important of all, interesting to themselves.

Making Meaningful Writing

It is possible that my view of writing and the conditions under which it best happens is idiosyncratic. Fortunately, researchers Michele Eodice, Anne Ellen Geller, and Neal Lerner interviewed more than seven hundred students at three different four-year universities, and they compiled their findings in *The Meaningful Writing Project: Learning, Teaching, and Writing in Higher Education*.[1]

Their findings suggest that college students are not so different from college instructors or professional writers when it comes to what we need to do our best work.

Students find writing most meaningful when they have some agency and control over what they're writing about. Freedom seems important to writing well.

Students find writing meaningful when they view it as a "social act," as part of an "environment" much larger than the assignment. In other words, students are more engaged when they believe the writing has a place in the world beyond school or an assignment.

Students find writing meaningful when they understand how the writing fits inside the larger picture of their lives and experiences. In the words of one study respondent, an environmental science major, "This is a subject that is important to me and that I chose independently. Hopefully, this will help me with my future employment as well."

In *Air & Light & Time & Space: How Successful Academics Write*, Helen Sword found similar attitudes among college faculty. Sword discusses the importance of the writer's BASE—(B)ehavioral habits, (A)rtisanal habits, (S)ocial habits, and (E)motional habits—for successfully producing writing.[2]

Under social habits, Sword articulates the importance of writing for and with others, writing as collaborative communication. Emotional habits include cultivating pleasure as well as learning to navigate risk and resistance, traits that extend well beyond writing.

The principles of what works when engaging with writing seem to be identical, regardless of status or experience. More experience may increase the writer's knowledge and confidence, but the challenges never go away.

I believe we should let student writers work under the same conditions as any other writer. If we want students to learn to write, they must work at building their writing practices. We should create as ideal an atmosphere as possible for them to do this.

This does not mean smoothing the path or removing all obstacles.

It does mean using obstacles that are conducive to developing the necessary aspects of the writing practice.

On cooking shows such as *Top Chef*, early on in the competition the challenges often involve removing something from the list of ideal conditions as a way to test the mettle of these very accomplished contestants.

The "quickfire" challenges constrain the competitors with time, forcing shortcuts, or, for example, asking chefs to execute something tasty from items found only in a vending machine. The best chefs rise to these challenges and produce something at least edible, but in very few cases is it their "best" work, and in many cases professional chefs with their own restaurants produce inedible food. Those sorts of failures will help inform future success.

But in some seasons, as the finale approaches, it's interesting to note that the final three chefs are given a month or more to go home and prepare for the last meal, and they are provided the use of their vanquished opponents as sous chefs to help prepare the food.

The judges seem to want to experience an example of what these chefs can do working under the most promising conditions because the goal is to produce and consume excellent food.

In the so-called real world we're often required to make compromises or sacrifices that stand in the way of our best work. Regardless of the necessity of those compromises, it is important to establish the ideal of at least knowing the target we're aiming for. That way, if compromises must be struck, we can understand how they have an impact on our ideal so we can perhaps compensate in other areas.

We know a good deal about the circumstances and conditions under which writers thrive, not only in terms of producing sound writing products, but in building their writing practices over time.

The most important value to helping students develop as writers is requiring them to make choices rooted in a genuine rhetorical situation that includes message, audience, purpose, and medium.

Rather than thinking of writing through the lens of "assignments" or "proficiencies," I believe we should be providing students with writing "experiences" that give them room to exercise choice and engage their intrinsic motivation.

And we should be using these experiences to help students build their writing practices.

Believe it or not, I first experienced this in third grade. It's only taken forty years for me to realize its importance.

Writing Experiences

What I Learned in Third Grade

Before going any further, I'm going to ask you to do an assignment first given to me by Mrs. Goldman, my third grade teacher, that I've since adapted into an assignment of my own that I use early on in my writing classes.

How Do I Make a Peanut Butter and Jelly Sandwich?

You may be thinking this kind of thing is beneath you. That's fine. Continue to believe this if you must.

But do this anyway. Consider it a warm-up.

PROBLEM

Someone wants a peanut butter and jelly sandwich, but they don't know how to make one. You need to tell them how to do it because they are hungry and peanut butter and jelly is good.

PURPOSE

To provide your audience with a piece of writing that allows them to satisfy themselves with a delicious peanut butter and jelly sandwich.

PROCESS

Write directions for making a peanut butter and jelly sandwich.

I've left space for you to do it right here.

We'll come back to this soon. For now, I shall tease you by declaring that hindsight has revealed the peanut butter and jelly exercise as the most important piece of writing in my life.

I believe that to help students write better, we not only need to abandon the five-paragraph essay—we need to get out of the "essay" business entirely.

When college instructors say, "Write an essay" (of the academic type), we usually envision something with an argument at the center supported by relevant and compelling evidence drawn from authoritative sources while adhering to the specific conventions of our field. Ideally, students are able to synthesize and even build upon an array of sources to create an original piece of knowledge.

When students hear "essay," they think: Five paragraphs, written to impress teacher, mostly to show that the student has been paying attention in class and/or doing the reading. Make sure to cite sources because . . . plagiarism. Also, use block quotes because that looks good and eats up the word count. Don't forget the conclusion that summarizes everything, starting with, "In conclusion." Never use "I." Contractions . . . bad. Why? Too informal? Why is informal bad? Because . . .

This is why most "essays" are unpleasant for students to write and boring or frustrating for instructors to read. They are treated not as an occasion to discover something previously unknown—to the author, above all—but a performance for an audience of one, the teacher, one hoop among many to be jumped through as part of the college grind. Following the high school grind, students are so versed in this pattern they do it on autopilot, and college instructors like me grouse about "kids these days" and their lack of dedication to their work.

Rather than allowing students to see a writing task as familiar to the point of being rote, I want them to approach each writing occasion from scratch. Every writing occasion is a new problem to solve, a new experience, and a chance to explore and improve one's practice.

Writing instructions for making a peanut butter and jelly sandwich in Mrs. Goldman's class proved to be quite an experience.

I have asked many hundreds of unsuspecting people to write instructions for a peanut butter and jelly sandwich, ranging from college first-year students to tenured faculty, and regardless of experiences or accomplishments, they do roughly the same thing. A typical effort looks like this:[1]

1. Get peanut butter, jelly, and bread.
2. Take peanut butter and spread it on one piece of bread.
3. Spread jelly on other piece of bread.
4. Put peanut butter side and jelly sides together, cut in half on diagonal.
5. Enjoy!

Mrs. Goldman did something interesting I've never had the guts to try with my adult audiences: she had us attempt to make our sandwiches following our own directions to the letter.

It was ugly, but if you are in third grade it's an awful lot of stupid fun. Looking at my typical example, we can quickly see how taking the instructions literally causes problems.

When the instructions say to spread the peanut butter on the bread they fail to give two important bits of information: With what? and How much? Mrs. Goldman had us spreading the peanut butter and jelly with our hands because we hadn't included knives in our instructions. If we hadn't specified amounts, she would have us keep adding more and more until she'd decided it was enough.

Mrs. Goldman was a great teacher. We loved her, and we shouldn't begrudge a grade school teacher occasionally using students for her own entertainment.

After we finished making our largely inedible sandwiches, I had my first inkling about what writing meant: *There's a reason we do this. It's for the people who need it.* But when I ask first-year college students *whom* they were writing for when doing their high school essays, they invariably say "the teacher."

But writing to impress a teacher to earn a grade and writing to fulfill the demands of a full rhetorical situation are different. When I ask people to write their peanut butter and jelly instructions, I leave out an important reminder: the existence of an audience. While the occasional well-trained writer understands an audience is implied when we create a set of instructions, the task is so mundane that most people simply forget instructions are meant to be used by someone who is not so familiar with the task.

The result is not instructions so much as a general description of the writer making a sandwich. Steps are skipped, details glossed over. The writer envisions making a sandwich and writes stuff down, never considering that someone may have to use the instructions for real.

Pausing to understand the implications of audience to a writing task significantly alters the outcome. If we instead conceive of our instructions as an effort to ensure someone makes the best peanut butter and jelly sandwich possible, we should probably add some information: in addition to utensils and amounts we should also include the type of bread, flavors of jelly, and varieties of peanut butter—crunchy, smooth, or that disgusting natural stuff where all the oil has floated to the top and they haven't added any delicious sugar. We won't just tell them to spread the peanut butter, but to spread it *evenly to the edges of the bread*. We may even offer choices, like trimming the crust, or lightly toasting the bread.

Audience awareness is one of a writer's key habits of mind. Audience analysis is a necessary skill. I have seen college students become alert to these ideas instantly upon using this very simple exercise, which takes only about ten minutes to execute. Once students see they have a more active role in the crafting of the writing, the dimensions of the writer's practice and their control over those dimensions come into view. It is unfortunate that so many students consider audience in their writing for the first time only when they get to college. This is a problem because our goal for all student writers should be for them to become self-regulating.

We Can't Teach Every Last Thing

As an instructor of a first-year writing course, I cannot possibly prepare students to write every sort of academic essay, let alone any other genre they may encounter in college. A history essay is not a philosophy essay is not a political science essay. Each of these genres may bear similarities, but they also have crucial differences that often are not articulated to students. I believe these disconnects account for much of the frustration faculty experience regarding the writing abilities of students, as students often default to forcing the square peg they know (including the five-paragraph essay) into the round hole of whatever they're doing.

When confronted with a writing occasion, students should be able to determine the dimensions of audience, purpose, message, and genre in order to fully understand the rhetorical situation. Once they understand it, they should employ a flexible and robust writing process that allows them to fulfill the needs of that particular rhetorical situation. This is a writer prepared to practice individual agency when confronted with any writing task, no matter how unfamiliar.

By insisting that each assignment be unfamiliar, I hope to short-circuit any impulse to follow previously employed templates. I want students to stop thinking about rules and start thinking about values as they make choices. I want them to ask themselves questions like, "Can I get away with a phrase like 'telling shit from shinola' in a book from an academic press?" Is profanity beyond the pale? What about the saying itself? Is it archaic? Have I included it to amuse myself or does it genuinely advance my argument and enhance my connection to the audience?

Students still write essays; I just don't use the word essay if I can possibly avoid it. Over the course of the semester, as we tackle different experiences, students recognize overlaps and see how techniques—or moves, as I prefer to call them—manifest themselves in different writing-related problems. Recognizing these overlaps is a good thing, as they work toward a self-knowledge about writing transfer—the ability to employ knowledge learned in one situation in an entirely different one.

To begin to turn student writers into writing-related problem solvers we need to substitute new values for the old. Rather than standardization, efficiency, and proficiency, we should be concerned with choice, curiosity, risk, and the building of a critical sensibility.

Each writing experience contains the following dimensions:

1. A question the writing seeks to answer
2. The problem that will be solved by answering the question
3. The audience for whom the writing is meant
4. A process that will lead toward an answer
5. A reflection that will help reinforce the metacognitive dimensions of learning and lead toward transfer of writing knowledge from occasion to occasion

Leaving the audience out of the peanut butter and jelly instructions lures students (and anyone else for that matter) into the trap of not thinking about audience and therefore writing substandard instructions.

Unlike common school assignments, which tend to reinforce highly similar skills from one assignment to another as students strive for proficiency on a fairly narrow task, different writing experiences may emphasize different aspects of the writing practice. The instructions for peanut butter and jelly are focused on audience awareness and the writing process. By inducing students into employing a writing process that fails to incorporate audience analysis, they will write poorly.

That's right: I have given my students a writing experience I want them to blow on purpose. It's actually quite enjoyable, as I learned from Mrs. Goldman.

Once the students have "failed" the peanut butter and jelly test, I give them the "reflection" portion of the experience, which is where the learning will actually happen.

....

How Do I Make a Peanut Butter and Jelly Sandwich?

REFLECTION

1. Exchange your directions with someone else.

2. Read their directions and imagine following them *to the letter*.

3. Would following the directions result in an acceptable sandwich? For example, is there a line something like this?

"Take the peanut butter and spread it on one side of the bread."

Picture executing the action exactly as described for a moment. What's missing?

That's right: What are they supposed to spread the peanut butter with if we don't mention the knife?

Something else is missing.

How much peanut butter should be spread on the bread? Ingredient amounts can be important in recipes, and my hunch is that if you do make and eat peanut butter and jelly sandwiches you're pretty specific about your own desired bread / peanut butter / jelly ratio. Why would you withhold that experience and wisdom from your audience, who may benefit from it?

You may be thinking that some of this is ridiculous, that of course someone would know to use a knife, and it's true, even an inexperienced peanut butter and jelly maker would probably know that a knife is used for spreading things in general, so it can be used for this task. On the other hand, what if they didn't? And if they do know to use a knife, what is the harm in reminding them in this case?

4. Go over the directions again, looking for any other spots where they could be more specific and clearer, or even more efficient.

One of the frequent problems you'll see is a missing first step, to gather all the ingredients together first. Failing to do this makes for a much more time-consuming process.

5. Also take some time to appreciate where the directions work well.

A good set of directions is probably formatted as a list, often even using numbered items. What other "moves" that are helpful to the audience are on display?

6. Take your instructions back from your partner. Utilizing their comments and now seeing your own work with fresh eyes after looking closely at someone else's work, rewrite your instructions into the best possible peanut butter and jelly sandwich.

Think about the necessary level of detail to really nail this sandwich. What kind of bread? What brand of peanut butter? What other details would make the instructions better?

7. Finally, think about the process (or maybe lack of process) you used in completing your first attempt at the directions.

What steps, if any, were involved in the writing of your directions? Did you plan? Did you think about your audience? Did you picture the task before you started writing? When you were done did you review or edit your work from the point of view of the audience?

How would you change your process in order to have generated a more successful set of instructions the first time around?

Rewrite the PROCESS portion of the assignment in a way that provides better guidance to a writer seeking to create directions for making a peanut butter and jelly sandwich.

....

I have spent many class periods patiently and clearly articulating the steps and stages to the writing process, along with the importance of brainstorming, audience analysis, planning, outlining, drafting, editing, polishing, and proofreading.

I have made these concepts crystal clear before students start to write their essays, and I have seen many of them ignore all of my good advice. But when I instead provide an experience such as writing instructions for a peanut butter and jelly sandwich and they see how lack of planning and process leads to problems, they learn more about the writing process than I could ever hope to convey by merely telling them stuff, no matter how true that stuff may be.

And here I have arrived at one of the other important experiences students must have as early and often as possible: failure.

Our Greatest Teacher

I have yet to meet the student who can successfully solve the peanut butter and jelly writing problem given the purposefully lousy guidance I give them. Their writing simply doesn't work . . . and that's okay.

Even more important, their writing is not scored by a teacher, but instead succeeds or fails based on how well it meets the needs of its audience, a standard students can judge quite competently for themselves through a process of reflection.

And even better, remedying the failure is within the abilities of the students themselves without any (or with very limited) instructor intervention.

If I were to grade this assignment using a traditional method, I would use their rewrite of the process portion of the assignment, because this is the writing most reflective of what students might have learned about the writing practice. But why bother even grading it? I don't care how good their instructions are for making a peanut butter and jelly sandwich; I care about what they learned in improving on their initial, likely poor, effort at writing those instructions.

In less than twenty minutes, I have seen students recognize more about writing as an act of communication than in the collective schooling they've experienced up to that moment.

When students are teaching themselves, they're learning. Even better, they're learning when a teacher is not present, the conditions they will be required to work under once they have finished their education.

Experience and Expertise

One of the most important criteria for writers to do their best work and therefore develop their writing practices is to be able to write on subjects with which they're knowledgeable. It is difficult to formulate ideas and engage in critical thinking if the material you are thinking about is unfamiliar.

Unfortunately, when students are learning to write, we generally require them to write about subjects about which they possess little knowledge, other than what they've recently gleaned from a limited number of texts or lectures. When the material is new, the best we can hope for is regurgitation of content, a lower-order thinking task which is also largely unmotivating.

One of the things we know from research into tests of reading comprehension is that performance on those tests is often correlated with how much the student knew about the subject prior to reading and responding to the passage in the test.

In a third grade reading test, when previously identified groups of "poor" readers were allowed to read a passage about soccer, the poor readers who already knew and understood soccer scored better on the test than previously identified "good" readers who were unfamiliar with soccer. The test was testing soccer knowledge, not reading ability.[2]

As the experiment reveals, decoding words and understanding the meaning and the message of a text are not the same skill. Context is vitally important.

The same divide is evident in writing. When a writer is searching for meaning because they lack underlying knowledge or expertise, the writing will be less fluent on every level. What looks like a problem with basic sentence construction may instead be a struggle to find an idea for the page.

Certainly part of the purpose of school should be building students' knowledge about subjects we believe to be important and with which they're unfamiliar. But if writing is thinking and thinking involves the expression of ideas, it is difficult to test student writing ability unless they are allowed to write (at least some of the time) from places of deep knowledge and expertise.

If we can identify ways to elicit student writing on subjects in which they are expert, students will become better grounded in the writer's practice. That grounding will also help them when exploring less familiar subjects, as they will come to know the gaps between occasions where they are confident in what they're expressing and those where they lack knowledge and context. Identifying those gaps is the first step to filling them.

Allowing students to write as experts is an excellent way to introduce them to the writer's practice. It fulfills many of the ideal conditions, and it allows them to showcase their knowledge in tangible ways.

This next experience, titled, "How Do I . . . ?" will be recognizable as a very traditional form called a "process essay" or set of instructions, but I don't tell students that. Instead, I put them in the role of an expert, helping a newbie.

. . . .

How Do I . . . ?

Try to think of some procedure or activity that you're expert in. Maybe you make the perfect cup of coffee. Maybe you can sew a dress or dress a deer. Can you defeat that impossible level on some video game or tell someone how to play "When the Saints Come Marching In" on the harmonica? Everyone has some kind of expertise they're capable of sharing with the world. Someone also may have occasion to need that expertise.

PROBLEM

Someone needs to learn how to do what you know how to do, but you can't be there to tell them how to do it, so you have to write it out for them. By following your solution to this writing-related problem they should be able to successfully do what you already know how to do. For our purposes you can use only words and descriptions.

AUDIENCE

Someone who has never done what you're telling them how to do. However, they probably cannot and should not be a blank slate. One of the first steps will be to more deeply consider who your audience will be. Consider their needs, attitudes, and knowledge regarding what you're going to ask them to do.

PURPOSE

The audience has a need—for a good cup of coffee, to play "When the Saints Go Marching In" on the harmonica, or something else—and they have turned to you as an expert in helping fulfill this need.

Don't be shy about it. Be the expert you are.

PROCESS

1. *Spend some time inventorying your own expertise.* What are you good at? What do you enjoy doing? What do you take pride in?

2. *Select your subject.* What one thing do you think best lends itself to this particular writing-related problem? Why have you chosen that?

3. *Plan.* A good way of preparing to write the solution to this writing-related problem is to do the action itself while taking careful notes along the way.

4. *Audience analysis.* Who is your audience? We know their need (to do what you already know how to do), but what might be their attitudes toward the task? Excitement? Trepidation? Something else?

Additionally, what about their knowledge? What will they need to know or be able to do prior to engaging with your solution to this writing-related problem in order to successfully execute the mission?

5. *Find and analyze models.* Look for models that solve this kind of writing-related problem. Stay away from ones too closely related to your own task. You don't want to risk copying, and also, remember that you're the expert here. You don't want to be unduly influenced by someone else's approach that may actually be inferior to yours.

Look at how these models are formatted and structured. How do they begin? How is the information conveyed? What techniques and choices will you use in your own instructions?

6. *Execute.* Write your solution to this writing-related problem. Do any necessary revising and editing as you see fit.

. . . .

"How Do I . . . ?" is an act of translation, an offloading of knowledge the student already possesses into a document for the benefit of an interested audience. It is both straightforward (in terms of purpose) and highly complex (in terms of execution).

In order to properly execute the assignment, students must engage with one of the most important skills in the writer's practice, reading like a writer.

Reading Like a Writer

The close reading exercises that dominate schooling—including at the college level—train students to be decoders of textual meaning. Good close reading exercises will require some degree of analysis drawn from observations and inference, but sometimes it's as simple as recalling something straightforward and factual, something purely informative. When students read for this purpose, the underlying questions students grapple with are: "What happened?" and "What is the meaning of what happened?"

This is a perfectly valid critical thinking skill, but reading like a writer is fundamentally different. Writers must be able to determine not only what a text is saying, but *how* it says it. Step 5 of the "How Do I . . . ?" assignment, "Find and analyze models," requires students to read their example texts like a writer.

In the case of "How Do I . . . ?" the focus is relatively narrow, asking students to study example texts primarily for insights on structure and formatting. In a class context, this is often done as a group, in which I ask students what they "notice" about a model text. I want them to start at the level of observation, from which they can later draw inferences and conclusions. This is a process they will repeat with just about every assignment, many of those assignments significantly more sophisticated and requiring more work for the students to decode the particular moves of the genre.

For this experience, students tend to notice the following traits:

- The steps are written as a list, with one step per item.
- Each step is a command. (I tell students this is the imperative mood so they think I'm smart and really know my grammar, even though it's the kind of thing more useful in a *Jeopardy!* tryout than in writing.)
- It starts with an introduction telling you the supplies you need.
- You know what you're trying to do before you even begin.
- It tells you why you might want to do this.
- There are ways to check your progress as you go.
- If something is extra-important or tricky, the steps include cautions.
- It ends with a way to see if you've done it right.

Following the observations, students are able to draw inferences about their audiences, the kinds of things they can assume audiences know or will be able to do without additional instruction. For example, a recipe may tell the user to "sauté" onions, but an entirely novice cook might not know what sauté means, indicating most recipes assume at least some familiarity with basic cooking technique.

Some may wonder why I go to such lengths to have students write something so straightforward as a set of instructions. Why not just cut to the chase, give them a template or an outline for proper instructions and have them fill in the template? There must be a shortcut, so why not take it?

Won't that lead to a superior end product? Quite possibly, but the product isn't the point. For students to learn, we have to make sure they're running over as many potholes as possible.

Against Shortcuts and in Favor of Potholes

For a long time I viewed my role as helping students shorten the learning curve.

Having made many mistakes during my own period of development, I believed I could aid students in avoiding potholes into which I'd once fallen and speed them along to proficiency. This involved lots of prescriptive teaching: do this, don't do that, watch out for these other things. I disdained the five-paragraph essay, but I was nonetheless carrying on its legacy.

In a first-year writing course, this meant highly structured assignments in which students were essentially asked to work inside a template or rubric. The content and arguments would be theirs—a plenty difficult task, I thought—but I would give them significant guidance on the shape and dimensions of the container in which to place their ideas.

I believe this approach likely helped produce "better" writing in the context of the courses, at least as judged by the grade on the assignments themselves. How could it be otherwise? Having been kept safely in the boundaries thanks to my prescriptions, the chances for a total whiff were decreased.

Now, however, I know I was doing my students a disservice. The assignments may have been better, but this did not necessarily reflect their overall growth as writers. I'd short-circuited some aspects of their development. What was going to happen when the man with the prescriptions wasn't available?

Believing I was shortening students' learning curve merely meant I was creating gaps in their writing practices by circumscribing choices. They were clearly learning less, which became apparent over time. I decided I needed to make a change. My role as the instructor shouldn't be to help students avoid potholes, but to help them understand what happened to put them into a pothole so they could avoid doing it again in the future.

My goals for students were too low, settling for proficiency rather than insisting on a process directed toward consistently and continually building expertise, not only in the class but beyond. I now recognize that deep learning, lasting, transferable knowledge, requires each individual to reinvent the wheel for themselves. Previously, I was giving students not just the wheels, but the entire car to go with them. At best, they were buying the gas.

I can declare some general truism about what makes a good piece of writing, but until students discover this truism on their own, often by doing the opposite and seeing the negative result, it tends to have little impact.

Exploring the writing process by inducing failure in the peanut butter and jelly instruction is one example of how potholes create more opportunities for learning.

This has the benefit of being true to how writing works in the world beyond school, but the structure and demands of school often make it hard to resist the lure of aiming for proficiency and smoothing the path toward that goal. Proficiency is simply an unworthy goal.

This means letting students make many of the same mistakes I've already experienced. The "reflection" portion of the "How Do I . . . ?" assignment helps students identify some of the potholes of this particular experience while working in collaboration with their colleagues.

....

How Do I . . . ?

REFLECTION

1. *Exchange with someone else.* If possible, have them attempt the task following your directions while you do the same with their task. If that isn't possible, do your best to visualize the process.

Would you be successful? Where might you be confused or even lost? Identify those sections.

2. *Think of a better way.* Writing instructions using text only was probably hard to do. What could be done differently if you had the benefit of illustrations? Looking at your colleague's effort, where would you especially appreciate an illustration?

3. *Think of an even better way.* Would your task be better learned with a different method? What about a video or other visual simulation? What would be the tradeoff between text instructions and video instructions? When is one more important or useful than the other?

Or is your task something that would best be done in a live setting, either one-on-one with you as the expert, or in a class setting? How would the different atmospheres change the learning? How would your role as the expert change?

4. *What's best?* Given total freedom to craft a solution to this problem, what method would you use and why? How and why is this best for the audience? (The solution may even be a combination of methods.)

. . . .

Once students embrace the idea that they are solving writing problems by engaging with writing experiences, my role as the arbiter of what is or isn't correct becomes unnecessary.

This is doubly good because the ways students have been conditioned to respond to instructor feedback are often deeply dysfunctional. Directing them toward self-regulation is a necessary component of their development as writers.

Learning from Your Mistakes . . . and Your Successes

"Why won't they read the comments?"

This is one of the most common laments of writing teachers everywhere, one I've expressed both out loud and internally over the years, as well as on student work—*Did you read the comments?*—sometimes with several exclamation points at the end instead of that question mark.

Here I was, spending hours casting pearls before my students who insisted on acting like swine. Addressing the shortcomings revealed by my comments would be the most important step toward improvement, and yet most students would flip to the end, look at the grade, and promptly move on.

I assumed that my students would transfer what they'd learned from one assignment to another, but this clearly wasn't happening. Identical errors would show up time and time again. Even small things, like making sure commas are tucked inside quotation marks (as is standard in American English), would be consistently missed by the same students over and over, even after I'd marked the error dozens of times over the course of the semester.

Did I ultimately start to threaten (only half-jokingly) failure if anyone failed to put their commas inside the quotation marks? I did. I'm not proud of it, but I did.

Did that help? Absolutely not. Would it have helped if I'd followed through on the threat and just failed students for what is admittedly a trivial and easily fixed error?

Definitely not. I could have gotten temporary compliance with my dictates, but there's little chance students would have learned much other than "commas really irritate that guy."

Beyond frustration, I started asking students, "Why don't you read the comments?" The initial response was often a shrug, as though they hadn't really thought about it, but upon further probing and discussion it became clear that the letter grade was the most important piece of communication. The comments, if they were reviewed at all, were mostly to see what I'd said to justify the grade. In some cases, students were looking for points to argue in search of a case for an upward adjustment, but even this was relatively rare. Mostly it was passive acceptance, a skimming of the judge's rationale for the verdict, which didn't really matter next to the sentence (grade) itself.

I was reluctant to be too hard on my students for these attitudes, because I had once exhibited the same attitudes when I was on the other side of the desk. I took another look at my comments, this time asking myself if they were really worth reading. If they were read, what would students walk away with that might be usable down the road?

Even the most generous interpretation revealed that, by and large, the comments were not particularly worth reading, as they focused almost entirely on all the things students did wrong. Very little of my commentary was focused on their next attempt. I'd been assuming students would pick up on the need to transfer what they'd learned from their mistakes simply because I told them they'd made mistakes. Not helpful.

In teacher-speak, my comments were almost entirely summative (here's what happened), rather than being formative (here's what we can do about it). This recognition transformed my approach to how I would come to use grades and frame my comments (which I'll discuss later), but it also caused me to realize students needed to be tasked with finding their own mistakes, because the worst thing a student can say after turning in an assignment or taking an exam and being asked, "How'd you do?" is "I have no idea."

I'm not talking about the inevitable niggling of uncertainty when your work is being assessed by another, but an experience of genuinely not knowing or understanding the criteria by which you're going to be judged.

If you're in over your head or lost, at least in theory there's a destination that could be aimed for. But if you're clueless about what you're even supposed to be doing, you drive in circles. In speaking with newly matriculated college students in my first-year writing class, many of them report having written something in high school they thought was good but then received a low grade. When I ask what happened, they respond along the lines of "I guess the teacher didn't like it."

Students who experience this kind of disconnect often feel they followed the rules under which they were asked to operate, and when the grade comes in lower than expected, they figure they must have missed one of the rules, or worse—the teacher is acting arbitrarily when they go to enforce the rules. When students lack a big-picture concept for what a piece of writing is expected to achieve in terms of a given rhetorical situation (audience/message/purpose/genre), these disconnects happen.

It's like trying to teach basketball by giving a list of rules—there must be five players per team on the court at any given time; there are four fifteen-minute quarters; you may advance the ball by dribbling or passing to another player—without starting by telling players the objective is to score more points than the other team by putting the ball through the hoop.

Helping students become self-regulating is difficult to achieve when over and over they repeat a pattern where they are judged by teachers. To break this pattern, students must be encouraged to judge how much and what they're learning for themselves.

The Importance of Metacognition

The key to this capability in writing is to help students practice "metacognition." Stephen Chew, professor of psychology at Samford University, defines metacognition in a series of videos ("How to Get the Most Out of Studying") as "a person's awareness of his or her own level of knowledge and thought processes."[3]

In essence, metacognition asks us to reflect on how much we know and how we've come to know it.

As it turns out, despite having more than a decade of college teaching experience, and having published more than a hundred essays, stories, humor pieces, interviews, four books, and various other types of writing, at the time I was asked to start writing a blog for *Inside Higher Ed* in February of 2012, my metacognitive knowledge of my own writing process was mediocre at best.

I learned this because when it came time to start writing posts for a blog, I had no idea how to write posts for a blog. At the time, I was expected to post once a week, somewhere between 750 and 1000 words, and it would often take me four or five days of consistent effort to produce that single post.

I now write two posts a week, fifty weeks a year, and it's rare for a post to take longer than a day's work. A couple times a month a post will come together in less than an hour. In 2017, I published over one hundred thousand words on the website.

Certainly practice was a key to my improving, but more importantly, it was purposeful practice that helped build my metacognitive knowledge of writing.

Thinking more about my difficulties blogging and what I'd done when I didn't know how to write something in the past, I realized that I had done something similar during my postgrad school career at a marketing research firm. I had started in the typing pool but was soon asked to fill in for an ailing colleague and write a report based on a focus group. So I asked:

Who is this for? (Client.)

What does it do? (Summarizes participant responses and synthesizes responses into analytical conclusions based on original research questions so the client may ultimately make a more informed decision on marketing strategy.)

How does it do it? (Starts with background, summarizes response, finishes with analysis and implications going forward.)

Pretty quickly I demonstrated that I was proficient at writing focus group reports, which is how I was able to go from the typing pool to having an office with walls not quite to the ceiling in less than twelve months.

Still, it wasn't until I was confronted with blogging that I consciously recognized I possessed a tested and true method for transferring my writing knowledge from a familiar genre to an unfamiliar one.

So I examined the blogs I was already reading and I came to recognize how they worked. Many were similar to essays with which I was more comfortable, but the blog entries often raised as many questions as they offered answers. Ideas were allowed to be provisional, floating something out there as a trial balloon rather than a finished product. The style could be as informal as I wished, and most importantly, I recognized that blog posts could go live to an audience with a considerably lower level of polish than something you might find in a professionally published book. I didn't have to spend days polishing the writing. As long as the ideas were clear, some infelicitous sentences could slip through.[4]

I could publish a post without having worked out a conclusion to my own argument. Over time, I discovered that commenters could help finish my arguments for me. A significant portion of this book includes words and ideas I first tried out in that blog space, now repurposed for a different occasion and audience, refined over time. I recognized that a blog post represents a direct conversation with the audience, an invitation for an exchange of views, and often a work in progress.

Metacognitive reflection about writing involves asking what the writer has done and how they've done it. Building this purposeful reflection into a student's writing practice allows them to see the links between different writing-related tasks, even when those links aren't obviously apparent.

With the "How Do I . . . ?" assignment, which asks students to write instructions, one important experience may be recognizing when writing is an inferior choice for meeting one's communicative purpose. Rather than asking students to be passive executors of the teacher's plan, after which they get a grade, the assignment forces the students to recognize the necessity of making a plan of their own against which they can judge their own success.

Not only does reflection increase students' writing proficiency by increasing their metacognitive knowledge of their writing practices, but it serves to reduce the anxiety students associate with writing. By allowing students to be experts—not just content experts but also presentation experts—I fade into the background as they take charge of their own writing.

Increasing Challenges

One of the things students want to know about me early on in the semester is how big a "stickler" I am. From their perspective, they're trying to suss out how hard the course is going to be by ascertaining my degree of sticklertude.

But the difficulty of a writing class should not be rooted in how big a stickler the instructor is. Difficulty should be found in the degree students are willing to challenge themselves.

Self-assessment is a key to self-regulation: it should be built into every writing experience, and it shouldn't end even with an instructor grade. As part of the reflection, one of the final things I do with each experience is to ask students a series of simple questions that yield complex answers:

What do you know now that you didn't know before?

What can you do now that you couldn't do before?

How did you learn these things?

In essence I am asking students to reflect on what they've learned as well as the process by which they've learned it. Sometimes the learning will be rooted in a failure. Students may say something like, "I've learned that if I don't read the final version out loud to myself as my instructor recommended several dozen times, I might not find very easily fixed mistakes."

That result smells like victory to me. Rather than students deferring judgment over their work to the instructor, they're required to grapple with the results of the experience for themselves.

The reflection is designed to help students "transfer" the knowledge from one task to the next. This is particularly important when the tasks are specifically intended to engage new challenges while also building on the previous ones.

The next step is to make students build subject expertise where, unlike the instructions of "How do I . . . ?" that knowledge isn't already present.

To practice this, I ask students, "Should I . . . ?"

. . . .

Should I . . . ?

Should I go see that movie? Should I buy that app? Should I listen to this album or go to that concert? Should I read this book, check out that museum, or eat in that new restaurant?

Decisions, decisions everywhere. Important decisions. Your audience needs help in making one of these decisions.

PROBLEM

Your audience wants to know if something (music, movie, book, TV show, app, clothing, food, restaurant, concert, play, video game, and so forth) is any good. They have come to you for your opinion, which they will rely upon to make their decision.

AUDIENCE

Your audience is someone your age in roughly the same circumstances and having had similar experiences. It's not you, but people similar to you, your peers.

PURPOSE

You are helping them make the right decision *for themselves*, which makes for an interesting challenge. On the one hand, you're going to need to be opinionated. On the other hand, you're going to also have to be informative and persuasive, telling them what they need to know about your subject in order to make a decision for themselves, while also arguing your point of view about your experience with your subject.

PROCESS

1. *Choose your subject.* It should be something you've never experienced specifically, but also something with which you're at least a little bit familiar. You shouldn't choose a horror movie if you've never seen a horror movie, for example. A good subject intersects with your own

experience and enthusiasms, but it's important you haven't yet experienced the specific subject itself.

2. *Find models.* Find examples of solutions to this writing-related problem. This should not be difficult. You encounter them all the time. Rotten Tomatoes aggregates movie reviews. Every newspaper in the country reviews TV shows, restaurants, music, games, and gadgets. It's more difficult to avoid reviews than to trip across them.

3. *Study the models.* What kinds of information and background do your models share? How are they structured? Where is the author present in the piece of writing? On what criteria is the subject judged? How do the examples help the audience in making the decision?

4. *Experience your subject.* Make sure to take good notes on your experience for use as you write your piece. Consider whether your subject should be experienced only once prior to writing, or if it's the kind of subject that is best experienced multiple times prior to writing.

What are the differences in these subjects? How does this make for a different piece? What role does the audience for your piece have in these choices?

5. *Analyze audience.* Be particularly thoughtful in considering the dimensions of your audience's knowledge. What do they know about your subject? What might they need to know, and when will they need to know it?

6. *Plan and execute.* Do your thing. It's your process. Just remember your audience and purpose.

....

We should notice similarities to the "How Do I . . . ?" assignment in that I do not name this piece of writing what it clearly is—a review. Students do not need much time to figure it out, but as with all experiences, I want them analyzing what they are about to do through the lens of the rhetorical situation using the tool of rhetorical analysis, by reading like a writer. Even by identifying the genre as a review, they're further along toward success than if I simply assigned a review.

Their study of the models will require them to build an understanding of the form and function of a good review, what a review does, and how it does it. It is important for them to ask these fundamental questions, rather than providing them with answers. If my goal were to have them write the best possible review, I would give them a template and lots of hints and guidance.

But this should not be our goal if the larger purpose is to help students build their writing practices through reflective practice.

Remember potholes!

This assignment also introduces another mistaken notion of writing I want students to abandon as quickly as possible: the illusion of objectivity.

The Perils of Objectivity

One of the worst disservices done to students before they get to college is leading them to believe that their writing—academic or otherwise—should strive for "objectivity."

There are many reasons why students arrive with this attitude. Taking standardized tests—where each question has a single "correct" answer—certainly reinforces this belief. Learning writing through rules and rubrics also communicates there is but a single path to be pursued. For many students, much of their school experience is rooted in parroting the official, existing body of knowledge enshrined by one authority or another.

Higher education too can make a fetish out of "objectivity" and "rationality," as though the goal of becoming educated were to achieve a Mr. Spock-level of dispassion, capable of purely rational and logical thought.

Please know, I am not anti-truth. In fact, truth is what writing should strive to achieve. But I am suggesting that pursuing truth is a process, a means without a definitive end. As we've seen in recent American politics, for instance, a wish to appear objective, often through the use of false equivalences, obscures rather than reveals truth.

There is no such thing as purely "objective" research. The work is inherently subjective, starting with the very choice of what to research. Those who get away with claiming "objectivity" in their research are more likely simply working in a kind of default mode. Anyone who falls outside the default is therefore violating the "rules," but peeling back these rules often reveals various instruments of compliance and control to protect a status quo, rather than a process that achieves "objectivity."

When someone claims the mantle of objectivity for themselves while complaining others are not capable of such feats, it's usually because the person claiming objectivity represents an established order that may be under threat by new ideas.

In these matters, "objectivity" is in the eye of the beholder. When somebody tells me a school is successful because they're improving on standardized tests, they aren't being objective. The values and ideology underneath the claim are simply unexamined. They are assuming standardized tests are a worthwhile measure of school improvement, a notion that should be contested.

Fortunately, because I teach writing, I can wash away student anxieties about being "objective" pretty quickly by reassuring them that it's impossible to achieve in their work, and they don't want to anyway because no one actually likes to read "objective" writers or writing.

I tell students they're after something better and certainly more stimulating for them than objectivity: "discovery."

When I assign a review in the form of the "Should I . . . ?" assignment, I enjoy watching students squirm as they realize they have to make an argument, and this argument is going to be based on their subjective experience and opinion.

On the one hand: Fun! On the other hand: What's the right answer? This is the kind of cognitive dissonance a teacher can work with. As students analyze the review genre they recognize there is no single answer to be found in a review.

Even the worst movies (hello, *After Earth*) have a handful of champions.

We discuss the fact that while they don't need to be objective in their reviews, they had better be convincing. Here we begin to talk about the values that underlie some example reviews as well as the kinds of reviews and criticism they most respond to as an audience. A lot of people enjoy opinionated reviews, but students recognize that those opinions carry more weight when they're accompanied with enough information for the reader to understand the basis of the reviewer's opinion.

Students make note of the rhetorical move of "positioning," where the reviewer quickly orients the audience to their particular predilections, like being a fan of a genre or director. Students see that agreement isn't necessary to appreciate a good review, and in fact, the best reviews may be best because they're the most fun to disagree with, as long as they are well articulated and sufficiently evidenced.

Worries about achieving "objectivity" quickly fade as we're now more concerned with values like "openness," "transparency," "fairness," and "accuracy." Students recognize a need to gain the audience's trust and speak with authority likely grounded in those earlier values.

Different audiences may require different choices of evidence: what is included, what is emphasized, how it's framed.

The review is a good warm-up for other more academically minded writing-related problems, as students practice employing the ethos, pathos, and logos—the ethical, emotional, and rational dimensions of discourse—that we will use in more formal argument. Rather than writing to please an authority like a teacher by demonstrating a fealty to rules that often seem disconnected from the writing itself, students are immediately in the knowledge construction business for the benefit of an interested audience. They must own their opinion, rather than offloading it onto a secondary source or outside "expert."

We discuss how their goal is to express things they believe to be true while recognizing that if they want others to agree with these truths they must practice the values (openness, transparency, accuracy, empathy) that undergird writing that connects with an audience. Perhaps more importantly, they must also practice these values on themselves, not as a way to achieve objectivity, but in order to know themselves and their "biases" better.

I use a different word than "bias," though, because I don't want them necessarily thinking of these things in a negative light. Instead, I substitute "beliefs." Strong writing comes from a strong set of beliefs, beliefs rooted in personal values. Those underlying values tend to be relatively immutable.

Beliefs, however, can change even as our values remain consistent. An effective writer is confident in communicating their beliefs, while simultaneously remaining open to having those beliefs challenged and then changed as they realize their existing beliefs may be in conflict with their values. This book, for example, reflects a process of bringing my beliefs about how to teach writing into better alignment with my underlying values.

When we encounter claims of "objectivity," I think of one of two things: either the person claiming objectivity is kidding themselves, or they're trying to put one over on me. In this context, "objectivity" is not a value, but a performance, and one that's usually viewed by students as phony. They easily recognize it as a confidence game because it's a game they'd previously been trying to play, and even then they knew it was a pose.

If we want students to be well armed for the world, they don't need to achieve objectivity, but instead require a "critical sensibility" that has been tested and remains adaptable to new situations and demands. Students shouldn't feel like they have to have all the answers. Rather, they should have the skills, knowledge, and experiences that allow them to tackle new and different questions. Sometimes answering those questions will require a change in their own viewpoints. For me, this is a core goal of education.

The primary emotion I witness students experiencing as they work their way through these writing experiences is relief. *So you're telling me I can say what I think?* It's liberating to know they have agency, which allows them to make space for their ideas in the world, even when that idea is limited to an opinion about the worthiness of a movie or an app.

When a writer believes they have something to say and is encouraged to say it, they will write better, and better writing is our goal. Encouraging independent thinking also prepares students for the kinds of critical thinking we expect in academic contexts.

Our new approach means requiring students to take charge of their learning through being empowered to write about subjects of interest and expertise, while also practicing self-reflection and self-regulation. This is the work of writers in the "real world."

But we can't ignore that these are students, and they're in school. Next we will explore how to bridge an assignment rooted in personal response (like a review) with the demands of academic writing, which require engagement with the ideas of others.

PART FOUR

Unanswered Questions

What about Academics?

Research Paper Trouble

The end of the semester is a trying time for first-year writing instructors. The cumulative weight of teaching, grading, and conferencing while often being responsible for too many students drains the physical and emotional batteries to a dangerous low as the term closes.

And then the "research papers" come in, and as you start reading through them, you may or may not burst into tears.

It's not the grading—though this is time consuming—so much as the crushing disappointment of seeing students who had made so much progress suddenly seem to regress. It's like seeing an ice climber who has reached the peak of the frozen waterfall and needs to drive the axe in just one more time to successfully summit, instead whiff on the swing, and tumble a good fifty feet down until the safety rope catches them. Nobody has died, but they aren't feeling so hot either.

The efforts very rarely "fail," but they are often disappointing, and from the instructor's seat, it can be hard not to blame oneself at least a bit.

Students are often as disappointed by their own efforts as I am. At the end-of-semester conference with each student, when I ask how they feel about their work, all the uncertainty I thought we had banished earlier returns. They recognize that the artifact falls short of the intentions—this is inevitable— but more worrisome is that many students cannot express how, where, or why it fell short.

The intention of the research paper was to produce an analytical essay with an original thesis that incorporates secondary sources. The essay should create knowledge, rather than merely report what others have said. This kind of essay requires the author's argument to take center stage, Gladys Knight to the secondary-sources Pips.

Unfortunately, few students are able to clear this bar, even when they had been building toward success earlier in the semester. There are many reasons for this failure.

In many cases, the first-year writing curriculum has shrunk from two courses to one. Trying to teach analytical writing from the ground up in a single semester while including a researched essay is enormously difficult. This is especially true as students arrive needing "deprogramming" from what an accountability-based system has done to them in primary and secondary school.

But the biggest reason students struggle with this final hurdle is because we underestimate the complexity of what we're asking them to do. In just three or four weeks, we are asking students to:

- Conceive a researchable problem
- Conduct research into secondary sources
- Evaluate sources for relevance, accuracy, and currency
- Develop a central thesis the essay seeks to argue
- Process sources at a depth that allows them to integrate secondary research into their own thesis rather than regurgitating someone else's ideas
- Draft, revise, edit, and polish the essay

When I employ this kind of plan, two months prior to initiating the researched essay unit, students are working on summarizing and responding to a single source in the form of academic argument. With the researched essay, I ask them to integrate as many as eight sources into an argument, sometimes requiring them to put two secondary sources in juxtaposition with each other.

This is a difficult task, highly dependent on not just writing skill, but existing subject knowledge and expertise. With the researched essay, over the course of a week and a half, I ask students to become conversant in a subject about which they might have been barely familiar as they began their library research.

It cannot be done in a genuine and meaningful way, and so students fall back on old patterns, including the five-paragraph essay, as they summarize each source one after the other, more laundry list of individual ideas than a coherent essay.

This is not a problem unique to students. Ask a seasoned academic to do something similar on a subject with which they're unfamiliar, and even with their superior skill and greater experience, they would struggle to produce something worthwhile.

I am not alone in my frustration with the research paper, and I am by no means first. In 1982, Richard L. Larson of CUNY, writing in the journal *College English*, declared, "I believe that the generic 'research paper' as a concept, and as a form of writing taught in a department of English, is not defensible."[1]

When Larson made this declaration, I was in sixth grade, with many research papers in my future as both a student and an instructor.

Larson argues that research should be properly viewed as "an activity," not a form or a genre. The generic "research paper" becomes a tool for students to prove that they can do certain activities, like locate sources in a library, or summarize them in an annotated bibliography, but those activities are often divorced from a larger rhetorical situation. The resulting research paper is a demonstration of having done those activities, as opposed to utilizing the tool of research as part of a robust and genuine analytical process.

Because of this, things like the correct form for citations

take precedence over allowing students to engage with original ideas. Students skim sources, looking for pull quotes, and arrange them in ways that resemble argument, but that are really surface-level glosses on a particular subject. At best, these efforts turn into "reports," a slightly more sophisticated version of what I produced in grade school when cribbing freely from the *World Book Encyclopedia*.

With the "research paper" as activity, originality is punished. Barbara Fister, an academic librarian at Gustavus Adolphus College in Minnesota, expressed her frustration when students bump up against the limits of the traditional research paper: "I hate it when students who have hit on a novel and interesting way of looking at an issue tell me they have to change their topic because they can't find sources that say exactly what they plan to say. I try to persuade them otherwise, but they believe that original ideas are not allowed in 'research.' How messed up is that?"[2]

The Citation Project, a collaboration designed to study student writing across multiple institutions, found that in doing research papers, in the words of one of the project's principal researchers, Rebecca Moore Howard of Syracuse University, "Students are not selecting authoritative, meaningful sources and not reading them carefully. They are not, in a word, engaging."[3]

According to the Citation Project research, 70 percent of student citations come from the first or second page of the source. Over half of the sources cited are cited only once.[4] I believe this because I've lived it, because I've assigned the research papers with prescribed lengths and numbers of sources, and I've dutifully introduced students to library databases. When I require an initial bibliography of sources before students begin drafting the paper, I have received many that simply list the first five (or six, or eight, or however many I've required) sources delivered by the database on their very first search of a single keyword.

Many times the bibliography includes items that are not

written in English, because students have not restricted their search to English-only sources. I can't think of a better indication of a pro forma effort.

But this is not a lazy-student problem. This is a bad-assignment problem.

Mea culpa.

The "research paper" is simply another example of education folklore. I used to assign one because that's what you're supposed to assign. This is college, and college is for academics, and the research paper is academic. Furthermore, other courses are going to make them write research papers. If I don't require students to write a research paper in my class, where the activity is supported, how can I expect them to succeed in non-writing classes?

But what if we're harming learning by making a fetish out of academic modes of writing that in reality barely exist, even inside academia?

Most educators and schools will say they wish to foster students' critical thinking abilities, while implying that traditional academic study is the best way to do so. But in assigning the first-year writing research paper, it is clear that I was not helping my students develop their critical thinking skills. If I assigned only research papers, my students would never learn to write an accomplished piece of researched writing. I needed to unbundle the kinds of skills, and more importantly, the type of thinking that underpins academic work.

Got Them Citation Scheme Blues

As I thought about how to develop students' critical thinking skills, I began examining other aspects of folklore surrounding the research paper, such as academic citation using Modern Language Association (MLA) format. If you want to hear a roomful of college students groan, say the words "MLA format." (If you want to hear them moan like wounded animals, say "group project.")

I ask students what they understand MLA format to be.
The parentheses and stuff where you put the page numbers down.
The thing teachers want you to do to show your sources.
If you don't do it, you might be plagiarizing.

Most students are familiar with MLA format and have used it in the past, but very few understand the underlying purpose of academic citation. It's another one of those things to be done because the teacher said so, a toll to be paid on the academic road, where you have no idea why you're handing over your money.

You should hear the groans when I tell them that the citation scheme produced by the Modern Language Association is not a universal standard but is confined to the discipline of English and that they will have to learn other citation methods if they write researched essays in courses in different departments. To students it feels like a terrible bait and switch.

I am not against academic writing, but when academic writing is divorced from its underlying purpose of fostering critical thinking and building knowledge it is little better than a standardized test that requires non-genuine performance, rather than a demonstration of genuine learning. When discussing MLA format, students should not be thinking about parentheses and formatting, but should instead understand the underlying purpose of citation, which is to provide the sourcing that allows other writers and readers to follow the original writer's path.

Students should understand the role of citation in communicating argument and persuading audiences through the use of evidence. Instead, they're wondering if you need to use a "p." in front of the page number.

Paul Thomas of Furman University, a professor with more than thirty-four years of teaching experience, including both the high school and college level, recognizes this disconnect: "Students, I find, come to college with a distorted concept of the essay as a form (usually something akin to the five-paragraph essay and mostly an act driven by a prompt and limited to literary analysis). Students also tend to see MLA as a universal, not discipline-based, approach to citation and essay formatting."[5]

Instead of teaching "MLA format," Thomas teaches "citation as a concept in real-world essays" by focusing students on Internet-published essays utilizing hyperlinks for sourcing.

The essay is an argument requiring evidence, but the evidence must be linked. This need creates problems students must solve while considering the audience, rather than worrying about teacher prohibitions or disciplinary rules. Students must decide which words to link, as well as how to frame the evidence, knowing that many readers will not click the links.

Before they learn the intricacies of formatting in academic citation, Thomas's students learn how citation works as a tool to meet audience needs, rather than a bizarre and byzantine system knowable only to academics. The context Thomas provides is key for transferring citation strategies and tests of evidence to other contexts later in the semester.

Thomas offers an example of how we can teach students to write and think as academics do without bogging them down with the baggage they attach to academic writing. We can also do it in a way that keeps students from being suddenly overwhelmed and overmatched, as they tend to be when I assign my end-of-semester researched essay.

Scholarly without School

I believe there is a way to help students develop "scholarly" ways of thinking without staying tethered to the strict outlines of academic genres. By disaggregating some of those critical thinking skills and allowing students to practice those skills before throwing them into "academia," we can better prepare them for success in that arena.

For example, one of the skills students should be developing is the ability to make observations and draw inferences from

those observations. This is a core element of critical thinking—
the ability to look at the world and make interesting and valid
conclusions from what we see. I introduce this skill through an
experience I call "Who Are They?"

....

Who Are They?

The figure below is a picture of some keys:

You can tell a lot about a person by their keys. Imagine these keys
have been left behind by a "person of interest" to a crime and you have
been hired to do a profile of this person in order to better understand
who they are, as well as their attitudes and beliefs. Assume that any identifying information that could lead the authorities to this person has
been exhausted. All we have are the keys and whatever you can glean
from them.

This is how Sherlock Holmes works to solve mysteries: he makes observations no one else can see and then draws inferences from these "hidden" observations. Your next experience is to practice this method, not to solve a mystery, but to understand a person . . . and to see the limits of observations in drawing those conclusions.

PROBLEM

Based on very little information, you need to try to describe a person who is a stranger to both you and your audience.

AUDIENCE

A nosy, curious person who is looking for insights into the subject of your study. Think of them as a client.

PURPOSE

The purpose of the writing is to catalog your observations and inferences in a way that will be understandable and accessible to your audience.

PROCESS

1. *Observe.* Spend about ten minutes looking at the keys. Write down as many different observations as you can. Observations are directly observable facts, such as: there are two regular keys, two car keys, and one keychain. Don't make any judgments about these observations; simply observe. While you're observing what is there, you should also be thinking about what's absent. What sorts of things that people put on keychains might be missing?

2. *Draw inferences.* What conclusions can you draw based on your observations? Who is this person? What is their gender? What do they like? How old are they? What do they do (or not do) with their time? What are their attitudes and beliefs?

3. *Extend inferences.* Based on those initial inferences, what other conclusions can you draw? What does this person do with their weekends? Who are their friends and associates? This will require speculation, but make sure it's speculation grounded in observation and earlier inferences.

4. *Report findings to client.* Consider an approach and format that delivers the information in a way that will be useful to your client. Be sure to be mindful of connecting your inferences to your observations so they can appreciate your evidence. Also, they'd probably like to know how much confidence you have in your various conclusions. What do you know? What do you suspect? What's merely possible? What's wild speculation?

5. *Compare notes with fellow investigators.* What did others see that you didn't? What did you see that they missed? Why do you think this happened? Are there inferences you disagree with? Where there's disagreement, hash it out through discussion. Which conclusion seems more likely based on the evidence available?

....

Students list many observations, including the number of keys and the fact that there are two car keys and a worn keychain from a particular college. They may note the lack of frequent-buyer cards for a grocery or drugstore. They figure out the cars are from Toyota and Fiat, and one of the "regular" keys is larger than the other. Doing this as a collective class exercise can generate dozens of observations in mere minutes.

These are my keys, and once the students have drawn inferences from their observations, it is amazing to see how close they can get to the truth of my life and identity, even if they don't have any idea that the keys belong to me. They're usually able to draw relatively correct inferences about my gender, age, marital status, alma mater, and relative station in life.

Students believe the subject is male, because they infer that women usually have much "busier" keychains, often with more tokens indicating individual personality, since women are more likely to carry keys in a purse rather than a pocket.

They believe the subject is married—though the more careful observers say "cohabitating"—because of the two car keys. Some will counter that it could be a fortunate young person with access to multiple family cars, but most believe the first interpretation is more likely, particularly if they search the keychain logo and find that this particular insignia has not been used by the University of Illinois since 2007.

The subject either owns a home (apartment dwellers often need multiple domicile keys) or has access to a home and an office, which suggests employment. To students, the fact that no discount cards are attached to the keychain suggests some sense of material wealth. (A more accurate inference is that I don't like so much of my personal information floating around corporate databases. Interestingly, this is an inference students almost never make.)

The point of the exercise is not to see how accurate students are with their inferences, but instead to practice "seeing" and helping students believe they're capable of generating original inferences simply through a process of analysis, without relying on an outside authority. The reflection also introduces questions of stereotyping and bias, how and when our observations may go awry, a way of building the writer's habits of mind of self-questioning and skepticism.

This skill translates to a later assignment with a more "academic" purpose, a rhetorical analysis of a humorous text in which students must answer the question, "What's so funny?" Students take on a humorous text, such as a bit from a stand-up routine or a comedy sketch, and are asked to move from a response, their own laughter, to observations (What did I laugh at?), to inferences (Why did I laugh?), to analysis (What does it say about a world in which this is viewed as funny?). Rather than deferring to "experts" as they're often conditioned to perform in traditional academic modes, students are building knowledge entirely under their own power.

One of the most important experiences for developing writing students is building that sense of empowerment and capability. When confronted with a question, we want students to believe they have both a process and a set of skills to employ to answer that question. Academic argument is particularly tricky, as students often recognize (generally correctly) that they lack standing to engage in the kinds of arguments we wish for. Cue the pseudo-academic BS. But we can and must derive ways for students to recognize and work through holes in their knowledge since this is an inevitable requirement for all writers. By asking them to perform intelligence, we're incentivizing the BS instead of activating student agency, which will drive them to fill in those gaps.

In teaching research and argument for much of my career, I've done things exactly backward, utilizing a well-worn process of having students choose a topic area, conduct research, produce a thesis, and then through some kind of alchemy, hopefully produce a coherent, original argument in the form of an essay.

As we've already seen, it often doesn't work. Students don't possess the experience or expertise necessary to take charge of the argument in that kind of situation, particularly when they're so inexperienced at arguing like academics.

This is why, when I introduce an argument, rather than skipping to an academic essay, I start with an "Impossible Argument."

I pose this question of my students: "Is a hot dog a sandwich?"

....

Impossible Argument

Some arguments are impossible to "solve." That is, there is no single answer that will be satisfactory to everyone because the "truth" is likely somewhere in the middle.

This may be true of all arguments, but let's not think about those other arguments for now. Let's think about an impossible argument.

Is a hot dog a sandwich?

Yes, absolutely? No, of course not? I bet you already feel passionately one way or another about this pressing issue and think those that differ are horribly misguided.

Good, let's argue.

PROBLEM

Convince the audience that your position on the question of "Is a hot dog a sandwich?" is correct. You must do this without relying on any outside research or additional sources. You will do it entirely based on your own experience and knowledge.

AUDIENCE

People who are interested and invested in this question, so pretty much anyone.

PURPOSE

To be persuasive. You want the audience walking away agreeing with you. At the same time, exposure to the argument should leave your audience in a greater state of knowledge about the subject than they were previously, even if they end up disagreeing with you.

PROCESS

1. *What is a sandwich?* If you're going to argue about whether a hot dog is a sandwich, it seems like you might first need to define what makes a sandwich a sandwich. Spend some time figuring this out.

2. *Is a hot dog a sandwich?* Now decide where you stand. You've defined sandwich. Does a hot dog fit the criteria?

3. *Argue the opposite.* What is the best argument *against* your position? Think about your arguments for your position and then imagine someone saying, "Yeah, but . . ." What do you say in response to their "Yeah, but . . ."?

4. *Write your argument.* Draft, revise, and edit a persuasive argument in which you come down definitively on one side of this issue. Remember, no sources allowed.

....

There are many different purposes to the impossible argument that relate to writing and thinking like academics:

- It introduces the concept of argument as a vehicle that seeks to illuminate and air differences not just as a battle between opponents, but as a way to help an interested audience make judgments for themselves.

- Ultimately, because the answer to the question is largely a matter of personal belief weighed against the evidence, students must get comfortable with the inherently ambiguous and provisional nature of academic work. They must take a stand and argue it as persuasively as possible, but they must also recognize that their stance may change based on new information. Many students end up reversing their original gut position as they work through the argument process.
- Students become "expert" without deferring to any experts. At the end of this process, students have a well-honed and defensible worldview regarding the status of a hot dog as sandwich or not sandwich.

To do the assignment, students must practice persuasion in the same way I will want them to operate in an academic argument. They must observe and draw inferences to form a central claim/thesis. They must be able to understand and refute counterarguments. They must attend to both emotional and rational persuasion.

They will become wholly convinced they are correct, and no amount of arguing with the opposite side—as I allow them to do in class—will convince them otherwise.

Sounds like the behavior of academics to me.

Once they're comfortable making an argument themselves, I allow them to bring in reinforcements through a reflection exercise.

....

Impossible Argument

REFLECTION

1. Try the argument again, but this time you're allowed to use outside sources to bolster your case. Where are you turning to for information? Why? What effect do you think these particular sources will have on your audience? What will be persuasive, and why?

....

Having crafted their argument initially without sources, they now can integrate sources, but their argument still remains center stage. They must do the work of source evaluation as they assess relevance and credibility. There is no distinction between the type of thinking students must do in this "impossible" argument and what we wish them to do in more obviously academic or scholarly arguments. Allowing them to do this kind of thinking without having to worry about being what they perceive as "scholarly" prepares them for a more scholarly approach.

But even when we get to something that will resemble a traditional first-year writing research paper, we can lead with student agency and student expertise.

Research Papers without Doing a Research Paper

I want students to have the experience of wrestling with a difficult problem and seeking to solve it through the writing. To do this successfully, they must be highly motivated to solve the problem. To achieve this motivation, I ask them to "get angry."

Writing about things that make you angry is an underappreciated pleasure. It may be one of my chief pleasures. It may be what's motivating this book, as a matter of fact. Students experience many discontents, both justified and less justified. I use those discontents as a route to get them to generate original knowledge using a process we recognize as "scholarly" in every sense.

....

"Why Am I So Angry?" (school edition)

PROBLEM

It's possible that I am a malcontent, but I seem to move through life finding lots of things I wish were different.

Schools for students of any age are often places of discontent, particularly for students themselves, since they are subject to so many different demands and often have little power. For years, I taught 8 a.m.

college classes, something I enjoyed, but something my students looked on as a form of cruel and unusual punishment. They figured they couldn't do anything about the existence of 8 a.m. classes except hope to schedule their own classes during other times.

But what if you could persuade those that do have power to make a change to that thing you hate? What if you could convince the people who schedule things like 8 a.m. classes that 8 a.m. classes shouldn't exist, not because students hate them, but because they do not fulfill the mission of the institution that schedules 8 a.m. classes?

Tackling a problem that shows itself in your school life is your next writing-related problem.

PROBLEM
Something related to school is not as it should be and you wish it were different.

AUDIENCE
Someone who has the power to make the change you seek.

PURPOSE
To persuade. But remember, it's not the persuasion of a small child throwing a tantrum until the authority figure gives in. You need to convince your audience that this change is in *everyone's* best interest, not just your own.

PROCESS
1. *Feel the hate.* Let loose all the things you really dislike about anything school-related. Visualize your day. What are the problems? What could be better? Write down everything you can think of, no matter how trivial it might seem, but try to focus on policies and procedures, rather than individuals. You're supposed to be in school to learn things and prepare for the future you desire. What stands in the way between you and learning?

2. *Find your focus.* From your list pick an item that seems important to you that also might be affecting others. It should be something that, if you can solve it, will have a positive impact on the school (or beyond).

3. *Consider your audience choices.* Who are all the different groups that are affected by this problem? List them. There will be many. We call these people "stakeholders." Which one seems both persuadable and able to make change? This is your audience.

4. *Analyze your audience.* Which decision maker(s) are you going to write to? Why have you chosen them? Consider their needs, attitudes, and knowledge of your subject.

5. *Make your case that a problem exists.* Write an argument that describes and illustrates the problem to the best of your ability without relying on any additional sources. This is based only on your experience, but remember what you know about your audience. What can you say that will persuade them to agree with you that this is a problem worthy of their attention?

You are not complaining. While you are working, feel free to feel your feelings and vent to anyone who will listen, but remember that in the end venting is a pressure release, not an effective method of persuading an audience to take action to help solve the problem.

You are persuading.

6. *Improve your case.* What additional information and research will help improve your argument that this is a problem? What do you need to prove to your audience to be convincing, and what kind of proof do you need to find? Are your sources convincing and authoritative? Or, maybe you've got a good case, but for a different audience than you first conceived. Should you switch audiences? Maybe you should seek out some test audiences to see how you're doing.

7. *Create a solution.* As you do research into your problem you will likely also find information on possible solutions. You probably have a few ideas of your own as well. What would be a good solution to this issue? How will you convince your audience that it's a good solution?

8. *Draft, revise, and edit.* Now that you've done all this thinking, planning, and research, write your solution to this writing-related problem targeted toward your specific audience.

. . . .

This assignment may take several weeks, and students will do a number of different drafts. As the culmination of a course that seeks to introduce and immerse students in the *how* and *why* of written academic discourse, it works for these reasons:

- By working from their own problems and experiences, students are writing from a place of expertise and belief— exactly what we expect of academics working in academia, and a necessary condition for doing one's best work, but one we too often deny students.

- Students are writing from a place of intrinsic motivation, another condition necessary to do their best work, and part of the writer's practice. The most enthusiastic students envision actually sharing their work with their real-world stakeholding audiences as they're working, and they often follow through once they're done.

- Students must engage in a sophisticated analysis of audience, often returning to their audience analysis several times over the course of the project. A significant number of students will write a first draft, recognize they didn't hit the originally targeted stakeholder audience, and need to adjust accordingly, either by revising their argument or changing their audience. Practicing reflection even during the drafting allows students to develop high levels of self-regulation, rather than trying to merely satisfy a teacher to earn a grade. They are thinking like writers.

- Using a problem-solution format allows students to take charge and lead with their own argument, rather than defer to their sources, as they're often tempted to do when confronted with a "research paper." If there is time, I give them a short, ungraded assignment that asks them first to "rant" about their subject, where they're encouraged to rhetorically let loose. Following the rant they usually recognize the limits of unhinged complaints in persuading others, and they adjust to making an argument that appropriately employs ethos, pathos, and logos, the base material of academic argument. Also, it's fun to write rants.

- The solution then becomes a way for students to work with sources in combination with their ideas without too much deference to those sources.

When students use their own experience to solve writing-related problems the results are simply better, and even when the writing artifacts themselves aren't as good as one might wish, students are still learning. They're building their writing practices, they're learning skills that will transfer to other writing tasks, and there is always an opportunity for reflection.

....

"Why Am I So Angry?" (school edition)

REFLECTION

How did that feel? One of the things you should experience in solving this kind of writing-related problem is the sense of your growing expertise. You will know much more about your issue at the end than at the beginning of the process.

In the larger world, this is how knowledge is built. You aren't hitting the reset button after every assignment, starting over in search of a new grade. The process never ends. Each act builds on the last until, without noticing, you seem to possess some real expertise on a subject.

Take a minute to list the things you know now, having written your argument, that you didn't know before.

Do you see how any of this knowledge might apply to other aspects of your life? Why? How?

....

It is a great thing to feel smart without having to rely on a teacher's grade to validate the feeling. Writing has the potential to be deeply empowering for students, not just as their skills improve, but as they increase their knowledge about the world, as well as their metacognitive knowledge of how they learn.

The sequence of assignments in this chapter is not the only route toward the goal. I have developed about sixty such assignments that can be employed for different purposes at different times.

I would be happy if other writing teachers adopted and used these assignments; underlying all of them is the important principle of providing students with experiences that help them improve their writing practices. The shape and tenor of those assignments will vary from class to class and instructor to instructor. We should remember the lessons of Christopher Emdin's "reality pedagogy" as we engage with different student cohorts.

I have no wish to impose a grand pedagogy, but I do believe that when we assign writing we need to be consistently more thoughtful about what we're asking students to do and why we're asking them to do it. If we focus on experiences rather than proficiencies, I believe students will learn.

Consider the writer's practice and what aspects of the practice a particular experience will engage. Not every assignment needs to engage in all aspects of a writer's practice. I have employed one experience where students in collaborative teams are asked to write topical jokes that you might hear as part of a late-night monologue. They almost certainly will fail at this experience, as judged by the quality of the jokes, because writing even a bad joke is very difficult.

But as an exercise in collaboration and attention to audience, students learn a tremendous amount through the experience, which can be completed in a single class period.

Enacting curricular changes to help students with their writing involves not only changing assignment design and considering pedagogical values, however. There are other ways we can help students develop their writing without falling back on the folklore.

⚘ What about Grammar?

....

When one of the chief complaints about student writers is their inability to make sentences that make sense, shouldn't this be a focus of writing instruction?

It has been this whole time; I just haven't explicitly laid out how. Grounding instruction in writing experiences rooted in the writer's practice while incorporating metacognitive reflection will result in student writers writing "better" sentences as a by-product of this process:

1. Having writers work inside a genuine rhetorical situation, most importantly including an audience, will eliminate much of the pseudo-academic BS, which is the cause of so many awkward or even nonsensical constructions. Giving students an audience helps them make choices grounded in purpose and message, rather than seeking to impress a "teacher" or perform "intelligence."

2. The rhetorical analyses of the genres within which students are writing means that they will not only read significantly more than students in a "typical" writing class; they will also read "like a writer," and that reading will translate into their prose. Students quickly learn to "imitate" the prose style of a particular genre, particularly when they've been immersed in that genre. This imitation will be significantly more readable than the pretending that happens when performing intelligence.

3. The reflective practice that steers students away from waiting for an instructor to tell them how they've done will make them much more careful crafters of their own

work. Grading standards rooted in reflection and process also increase this effect.

4. Activating intrinsic motivation, where students revise and polish because they want to do their best work and because they are engaging audiences, results in better sentences than writing produced under the threat of poor grades.

5. Simply put, students will be writing more words. By focusing on experiences, students may write thousands of words in a day. Sometimes these words will also be revised and polished. As long as students are writing, and writing with purpose, their writing will improve.

Still, there are times when we do want student attention at the sentence level to be more purposeful. Rather than teaching grammar, though, we should teach the skill we want them to improve: making sentences.

To facilitate this purpose, I teach a combination of "sentence appreciation" and "sentence manipulation."

In an example lesson, I introduce students to three sentences:

1. I have smelled what suntan lotion smells like spread over 21000 pounds of hot flesh.
2. I have smelled what suntan lotion smells like spread over 21000 pounds of hot skin.
3. I have smelled suntan lotion spread over 21000 pounds of hot flesh.

The sentences come from the opening passage in David Foster Wallace's essay, "A Supposedly Fun Thing I'll Never Do Again," which recounts his time on a Bahamian cruise. The first several paragraphs cover what he saw, heard, and smelled on the trip, including all 145 cats inside the Ernest Hemingway residence in Key West, Florida.

Sentence three appeared in the originally published version of the essay in *Harper's* magazine (under the title "Shipping

Out"). Sentence one is how it appeared in an author-restored version in DFW's essay collection that shares the title of the cruise ship story.[1] (It's worth noting that in the *Harper's* version of the piece, the author used the figure "2,100" pounds, changing it later to "21000" pounds in the version published in the book. In my class I simplified things by consistently using "21000" in all three sentences.)

Sentence two is my own variation.

In class, I start by reading aloud the opening paragraphs of the essay, which includes sentence one, asking students to make note of any specific details that strike them as they listen. The opening is riddled with vivid descriptions, including one of a "woman in silver lamé projectile vomit[ing] in a glass elevator," and "a tropical moon that looked more like a sort of obscenely large and dangling lemon than like the good old stony U.S. moon I'm used to." Almost without fail, "I have smelled what suntan lotion smells like spread over 21000 pounds of hot flesh" winds up in students' notes.

I ask them why.

It's so gross.

Why is it so gross?

Flesh. Flesh is gross.

By reading the passage out loud first, I'm seeking to provoke student responses. They can't help but cringe at the sentence and in doing so recognize its rhetorical effect.

I show them sentence two, and I ask them to compare it to the original version. Universally, they agree "skin" has less impact and "flesh" is much grosser. Here we pause to discuss his choice to gross us out. Shouldn't tanned bodies be attractive? Isn't this the expectation? Why does the author want us to recoil in horror?

What is the difference between "skin" and "flesh?" Students tell me "skin" is just the surface, while "flesh" implies something literally "meatier" that makes the people seem not human, but just . . . well . . . bodies of "flesh."

It's gross.

At this point, students have been exposed to about one-fiftieth of the essay, and yet they already clearly understand Wallace's intentions—his pose as a cruise skeptic. They know this is not an essay meant to immerse us in a comforting vision of rest and relaxation, but a critical look at the experience.

After this discussion I focus on sentence three, and here it gets really interesting.

I ask two questions: (1) Which sentence is most "correct"? and (2) Which sentence do they like the "best"?

1. I have smelled what suntan lotion smells like spread over 21000 pounds of hot flesh.
2. I have smelled what suntan lotion smells like spread over 21000 pounds of hot skin.
3. I have smelled suntan lotion spread over 21000 pounds of hot flesh.

Again, just about universally, students agree that sentence three is the most "correct" sentence. The repetition of "smelled" and "smells like" just seems "wrong."

And they're right, I suppose, but when I ask them which sentence they like best, somewhere between one-half and two-thirds choose the first sentence, which may be mechanically awkward, but at the same time has an oddly pleasing quality because of that awkwardness. It seems to fit the author's mood and experience to sound a little awkward as he's sorting through what was an apparently disorienting experience.

Some students prefer the *Harper's* version (version three) for its concision, which is fair enough. We talk about how the style of a magazine that publishes many different writers per issue but still needs to sound cohesive may require greater degrees of uniformity than a collection of essays by the same writer.[2]

As readers, students can be remarkably sensitive to changes and choices at the sentence level when they are required to attend to the text in that kind of detail. In fact, this is where the oversaturation of close reading in their primary and secondary educations can come in handy. It requires a little recalibration as they focus on their own responses, as opposed to trying to figure out the "right" answer, but the basic skills are present and can be worked with.

It can be more difficult to get students to pay attention to their own sentences, but this attention can be achieved as well without ever breaking out a grammar worksheet. Audience, intrinsic motivation, and sufficient freedom all help.

Early in the semester I invoke Mark Twain's dictum, "The difference between the almost right word and the right word is really a large matter—it's the difference between the lightning bug and the lightning." I want students to believe there's a better word to be had. They recognize that choosing "flesh" over "skin" makes for a significant difference.

The search for the right word affects the kind of feedback I give students on their sentences. Rather than focusing on deficits or correctness, I'm alert for "energy" and "impact." I highlight the passages that seem to work well, and I ask students what went into creating them. I may then contrast them with other parts that lack punch or clarity. A mechanically confusing sentence isn't marked as "incorrect" and then corrected by me. I may say it's "awkward," or I may say something like "cloudy," if the issues obscure meaning.

A correct sentence that has too many almost-right words and not enough right ones might be "flat."

In this way, I'm much more like an "editor" who is coaching the writer than a "teacher" who is identifying errors. Having done both jobs, I've come to realize that my "editor" self works better at helping writers meet their goals and improve as writers than my "teacher" self.

For developing writers, I also must temper my expectations for how often and to what degree students may nail their choices in the same way David Foster Wallace does in this essay. Wallace was one of the most revered and expressive prose stylists of his generation. We should not expect students to exhibit "genius" in their writing, but we should expect students to practice the kind of care and consideration Wallace brought to his writing.

Back to an earlier golf analogy. If you're a twenty handicapper, there may be three to five really great shots in an entire round. If a handful of moments in a student's writing absolutely sing, I point to those and say, "There it is. Do you feel it? How do we get everything so it feels like that?"

For the sentences that get hooked into the woods, rather than remarking about how very wayward that shot went, I ask the student, "What were you thinking with this? What are you trying to do?," redirecting the student back toward a reflective process under their own control.

Even though his cruise ship essay had been published in one of the most prestigious magazines in the country, David Foster Wallace revised it for the different context of a book consisting entirely of his own writing, not subject to editorial control. Rethink, revise, do it again. Students come to see writing as a recursive process without end.

We cannot grammar-drill our way to getting students to produce good sentences. Students must be motivated and empowered to pursue those goals on their own initiatives, with instructors on hand for encouragement or adjustment or the occasional stern warning as necessary.

The right word for their own writing lives inside the students themselves, not their instructors.

℞ What about Grades?

....

There's little dispute that grades do more harm than good in helping students to learn writing. It's no longer even up for debate.

Grades are perhaps the most pernicious example of education folklore.

As measurements of learning, grades are maddeningly imprecise. As traditionally used they do not reflect how much a student learned, particularly in a writing course that includes students who enter with different levels of experience and ability. The student whose writing moves from a D to a C+ over the course of a semester has learned much more than a student who entered and left with a B+, and yet in today's school world, that C+ student will be viewed as a failure and the B+ student a success.

Grades are actively demotivating when it comes to learning. Grades engage "extrinsic motivation," which can lead to what researchers as far back as 1977 called the "minimax strategy," under which students do the minimum required for the desired grade.[1]

I was the master of this approach in college, using a strategy that kept C's off my transcript at all costs, because C's were the threshold for parental ire. With no plus or minus grades, an 80 (or a 79.5) was the same as an 89 (or 89.4). My math skills got a workout as I calculated what I might need on an exam in order to cross the no-C threshold, but my knowledge of the subject at hand was not improved.

Even when students are already intrinsically motivated by a particular subject, the injection of grades will diminish that intrinsic motivation and result in less dedication and less learning.

Consider that for another moment: Imagine a child who enjoys playing the piano, who spends hours at the keyboard, listening to music and trying to play the tunes by ear. If you introduce a reward for something like time spent practicing or number of songs decoded, the child will spend less time playing the piano.[2]

Similarly, grades focus students on what they "need to do" rather than what they could do or want to do. Curiosity is less important than performance.

Grades incentivize cheating and plagiarism. Most students are not interested in conniving their way through school, but when students are staring at a failing grade because they haven't done the work—often because they're unsure of exactly what they're supposed to do—sometimes they will do desperate things.[3]

Grades are unfair. In a class using a traditional grading system with five assignments, each worth 20 percent of the semester grade, a student who gets 95, 95, 93, 93, and 70 is given a B, even though 80 percent of the work they did during the semester was A-level.

And importantly, from my point of view as an instructor, grading often distorts how I respond to my students' writing. When I feel obligated to justify a grade, I concentrate most of my effort on explaining "what happened," but if we want students to learn, we should focus instead on "what's next."

Studies comparing feedback of grades, comments, and grades combined with comments showed that students who received comments only were more likely to improve. Agency, self-regulation, and self-reflection are all diminished when grades are employed. Grades train students to defer their judgment to someone else.[4]

Grading has some value. If we want to rank and sort something, grades are useful. USDA grades on beef will not harm the quality of the product because the cow's work is already done. Under the right circumstances and when incentives are aligned, grades can be motivating. The restaurant that receives a failing grade on its health and sanitation rating will need to remedy the situation with all due haste.

But grades are antithetical to learning.

It took me a long time to come around to this view. Even though I had been suspicious of grades for many years, I didn't know there were different ways of assessing student work. I was captive to the folklore.

I have experimented with a dozen different permutations inside a traditional grading system. For instance, I have weighted every essay the same. I have allowed students to drop their worst grade. I have made the final assignment worth more than 50 percent of the grade, on the theory that it would be the best reflection of how much the students had learned by the end of the semester. Under this system, however, the additional pressure of performing on an assignment with so much weight ratcheted up the pressure to unbelievable levels, and all of the bad incentives of extrinsic versus intrinsic motivation kicked in to boot.

Finally, after years of dithering that would have made Hamlet look decisive, I committed to challenging my own ingrained patterns. My enlightenment came after reading the work of instructors/scholars such as Jesse Stommel, executive director of the Division of Teaching and Learning Technologies at the University of Mary Washington, who advocates for grading practices that emphasize self-reflection and agency.[5] If my goal for students was that they learn to write, grades are not only not helpful; they're actively harmful, and I had to do away with them.

But we probably can't do that. It would be wonderful if we could foster a sudden uprising of teachers and students throwing off the yoke of grades, and there is a nascent movement of teachers at all levels "going gradeless,"[6] but grades and assessment will always be a part of schooling.

If we're going to grade, however, I believe it should be done in a way that is consistent with what we claim to be our values.

If the purpose of school is to help students learn—rather than to sort students into their designated slots—we should be assessing them in ways that lead to learning. This can be achieved by first considering what is important to encourage student learning. What experiences and behaviors should we be stoking?

If I want students to learn as much as possible about writing, what sorts of things do I want them to do?

My answer? Read and write. How had I learned to write? Reading and writing, reading and writing. And then reading and writing some more.

In graduate school I wrote one hundred thousand words of fiction each year for three years—and I became a much better writer of fiction, while still finishing school as a not-yet-published fiction writer. How did I go from taking a week to write a blog post to taking a day?

Reading and writing.

I am a slower learner than most, but if my students were going to improve at writing, they were simply going to have to practice by writing lots of words.

I changed my assessment scheme. Rather than grading students on the "quality" of their work—a frankly silly notion in an introductory class to begin with—I would grade them on the volume of production. More work and more words would mean a better grade. I would establish different thresholds of the amount of work completed for each letter grade.

The work would still have to be purposeful. There was structure, there were assignments (experiences) and guidelines, and students would receive feedback from me and others, but at the end of the semester they would be judged on how much they did. More work, better grade.

More work, more learning.

Additionally, liberated from concerns of judgment and grades, their work improved. The resulting writing was more inventive, more thoughtful, and usually more polished as intrinsic motivation kicked in.

I was convinced students were learning more. Even better, students reported a shift in how they were viewing writing.

Students expressed their course-end sentiments in ways I could only have dreamed of ten years earlier:

> "This class was graded using a grading contract instead of normal letter grades per assignment. I liked this much better because it allowed for more freedom and room for growth and development during the assignments; I wasn't so focused on getting an A, I was focused on getting the most out of each assignment and enjoying the writing process."

> "I have learned so much in this class and it made me want to continue my journey with writing."

> "Learning was a pleasure."

> "Really brought out my inner writer."

> "I feel as though I really did grow as a writer."

> "I am a much better writer than I used to be, and I have a lot more respect for the act of writing."

> "I learned a lot in this class and am much more interested in writing now."

My judgment of student proficiency had finally become less important to me than increasing their desire to write and their confidence in their own abilities to improve as writers. As the semester progressed, I felt myself fading further and further into the background of the course. I was present and part of the conversation, but I remember one moment toward the end of the semester, when I had given students a lab period to use as they wished on their final projects. I looked around the room and saw something like a playground (or maybe "workground") the students had created and populated for themselves.

I wasn't necessary, which is how it should be. I cannot teach students everything they need to know in a semester. If students express confidence that they can continue to learn, I know the experiences I've given them and the way I've assessed their writing have worked.

I wouldn't suggest that every instructor borrow my grading contract wholesale and impose it on their course because it simply wouldn't work. Different courses and different student cohorts require different approaches. In certain contexts, such as a capstone journalism course where students are expected to produce print-ready copy, an emphasis on the quality of the final product may be vital. Spelling someone's name wrong in the story—a guarantee of an email or phone call to an editor—could be viewed as grounds for failing the assignment. But in that context, a grading contract that emphasizes that sort of judgment is actually consistent with the values of the subject and the course. Even in my own teaching, I see how and what I grade as a work in progress, often making adjustments based on student reflections about their own learning. As students tell me what they need in order to continue to improve, I alter course.

However instructors employ grades, it must be done in a way that is consistent with what we want students to experience and learn. Traditional grading systems often distort the values many instructors claim to find most important.

It is a journey that literally took me years, and it hasn't ended yet. But by questioning the folklore and collaborating with students on what they need to better learn, I started a conversation that requires students to be invested in their own learning in ways grades could never come close to achieving.

What about the Children?

. . . .

I do not have a copy of my birth certificate. I'm pretty sure there is a wedding license somewhere, but I haven't seen it since the wedding itself. I have zero scholarly artifacts from college save a fading and frayed photocopy of my transcript.

I no longer even have a physical copy of the first book I published, but for some reason I have the portfolio of writing I produced for Mrs. Minch's fifth grade class of 1980–81 at Greenbriar Elementary School in Northbrook, Illinois.

Bound between two sheets of laminated construction paper (front: orange, back: light green) lashed together by three strands of pumpkin-colored yarn fed through punched holes. It is imaginatively, yet also incorrectly, titled "12 Stories" because only six of the twelve entries are properly labeled "stories."

I imagine my future biographer digging through the archives I will have donated to a prestigious university library, finding "12 Stories," and scratching a note along the lines of: "Warner's future genius was apparent as early as grade school as he demonstrated a unique gift for language as well as plotting in the surprising 'When Joe Got Rid of Flo,'" reprinted here in its entirety:

> *Once there was a man named Joe*
> *Who had a girlfriend named Flo*
> *They went to a game*
> *Where Joe picked up a dame*
> *And that was the end of Flo*

I believe Flaubert also started his career working in the limerick form, but don't quote me on that.

In reality "12 Stories" reveals what appears to be a pretty average kid with an active imagination, terrible handwriting, and an uncertainty over whether "a lot" is spelled "alot" or "allot." (Never is it actually spelled correctly, but never mind.)

The specific curriculum and approaches toward building the writer's practice in this book are mainly focused on late high school and early college students. However, I believe it is never too early to plant the seeds that will prepare younger school-age children to successfully develop as writers and thinkers. If I convey nothing else in this book, I believe that it will be my hope we will recognize that writing and thinking are inextricably linked.

I am not suggesting grade school students across the country should simply replicate the assignments contained in my "12 Stories" portfolio, which, in addition to the opening limerick, includes a play, a riddle, a classified ad, original folklore, autobiography, historical fiction, speculative fiction, and that thing you can do in which you spell a word down the left margin and then list words starting with each of those letters in turn. This was my take on "Thanksgiving":

Turkey and all good things to eat.
Happiness and love to everybody.
All my loving animals.
Niceness, caring and food.
Kindness, cousins and aunts and uncles.
Skiing, snow, and Colorado
Greenbriar, Glenbrook, and other schools
Ice hockey, soccer, and other sports
Very nice moms and dads.
Ice cream and other sweets.
Nice people and teachers.
Grandmas and brothers.

That said, one could do worse than what "12 Stories" demonstrates in terms of the range of writing tasks I was asked to do and aspects of the writer's practice that were engaged by those tasks.

It's really a matter of embracing the same values that allow students to practice agency as they write for specific audiences under specific purposes. An unfortunate byproduct of our mania for making children "college- and career-ready" is pushing training and standardized assessments further and further down the ladder until they've even invaded kindergarten. But I believe our main goal for primary school should be for students to look forward to doing the work of school.

In her book, *The Hungry Mind: The Origins of Curiosity in Childhood*, Susan Engel of Williams College argues for the necessity of putting children's natural curiosity at the center of the classroom. Rather than using standardized assessments, we should be recording classroom activities and conversations, measuring how engaged and enthusiastic children are in school.[1]

In that spirit, if I became czar of all things education, up until sixth grade I would use a one-question test to evaluate academic progress: "What did you do in school today?"

The measurable data would be time, as in: How much time does the child spend prattling on about what happened in school? If you eventually have to cut the child off because you can't take anymore, you will know the child is having a worthwhile educational experience.

This does not mean pandering to children, unless we define pandering as presenting children with an interesting variety of challenges that will pique their curiosity. Remember that a majority of students from fifth through twelfth grade report either being "not engaged" or "actively disengaged," a percentage that rises each successive year. If we want students to be successful at school, we should give children work that is engaging. Expecting grade school students to grind away in the service of a goal—College! Career!—so distant as to seem illusory flies in the face of everything we know about how we best learn.

My fifth grade portfolio actually demonstrates writing tasks of significant variety and even sophistication. We think of limericks as silly, but the structure, with its strict meter and rhyme, forced me to manipulate language in a challenging way. I don't believe "dame" is a word you would have heard me casually throwing around because I did not grow up inside a 1940s detective noir film, but this small problem engaged me in ways a more straightforward, strictly "academic" task might not have. It's certainly more stimulating than prepping for a standardized assessment.

The classified ad, imaginatively listed as "For Sale" in the portfolio table of contents, is all of five lines on notebook paper, but—although I didn't realize it at the time—it forced me to engage with a writing task using all dimensions of the rhetorical situation: purpose, message, audience, and genre. I even had to read like a writer.

I needed to analyze the form to see what elements should be included, as demonstrated by listing the item first ("skateboard good condition green"), and finishing with my home phone number and "ask for John." The sentences are short and pithy—"Price, $4.25 or trade for something"—which befits the genre. Clearly I internalized how this kind of communication was supposed to work and sound. I could ask first-year college students today to do a somewhat more sophisticated version of the assignment and it would be entirely appropriate.

But it is another assignment from Mrs. Minch that I find most remarkable in hindsight, and I am going to steal it to use with my students. I do not know what the full prompt was, but it must have been something like, "Describe an invention and say why you think it would be useful."

My invention was the "Capulerari Acidizer Platizki Educationer" or "CAPE." Apparently, I wanted to use CAPE as an acronym so I made up some nonsense words. The CAPE was designed to help kids "learn in your sleep and put teachers out of business."

As described, the CAPE is something like an iPod programmed with educational content that is fed directly into the brain through "feelers" placed on one's forehead so the subject learns in their sleep. Thanks to the speed and efficiency of the CAPE, "you can go through grade school in one year."

All schooling is finished by age fourteen, after which you take "referesher [sic] courses," which presumably would include spelling.

It would cost $5000, "which is much less than the cost of an education."

I wouldn't mind a visit from ghost Marley taking me back through my life so I could see how Mrs. Minch reacted to this piece when I turned it in. Did she get a kick out of it? Did she stew over that "ungrateful little SOB?" I wouldn't have blamed her, but clearly, whatever her feelings might have been, she respected my autonomy enough to let me put these absolutely foolhardy, insulting, ridiculous ideas into an end-of-semester portfolio of my most important work.

Despite all the mistakes, there is not a single mark from a red pen in my portfolio. My memory is that these are revised versions, and Mrs. Minch had provided feedback on earlier drafts, which we were expected to incorporate into these "finished" versions. I hope I corrected some of the errors, though I suspect I introduced new ones. This is the artifact I was going to take home and show to my parents, the thing we're meant to keep. Marring it with corrections would have defeated the purpose.

With almost forty years of hindsight, and having spent so much of my life teaching, I feel great appreciation for the freedom I was given to express myself and explore my own mind, even as a young child. I was given assignments with purpose and audiences from my very first in-school writing experiences, like the "weekend news" we were to write each Monday in Mrs. Craig's first and second grade class.

I remember the giant newsprint broadsheet with lines for writing, including a dashed line to help with lowercase cursive letter height, and space for illustration above. Mrs. Craig asked us what we had done over the weekend and we told her. She was our audience and we wanted her to know about our lives. I hated the drawing, but I loved telling Mrs. Craig about my newest passion, playing ice hockey.[2]

In fourth grade, when we had an outbreak of bullying that manifested itself through name calling, Mrs. Thiel challenged us as a class to come up with a solution. We'd already been learning how to use and exchange money through a classroom economy where we were paid in class scrip, which we could use for weekly auctions of awesome stuff like erasers shaped like race cars or those rings that look like Halloween spiders. I had a brainstorm: insurance. What if you could use your class money to purchase insurance against being called a name? If you were called a name and could prove it, the insurance company would collect from the offending party.

(I'm aware this isn't exactly how insurance works. We were nine years old.)

In short order, I was co-running a name-calling insurance provider, and I was writing policies for purchase. The first attempts were failures. I thought it would be enough to simply sell the name-calling insurance, but then we found ourselves in disputes over what was or was not a derogatory name.

My friend Mike had a nickname, "Sluggo," based on a certain resemblance to the character from the *Nancy* comic strip. Lots of us called him Sluggo, intending to tease our friend, rather than be outright mean, but Mike didn't like it when someone who wasn't a friend used the nickname. (He probably didn't love it when his friends used it, but he tolerated his friends.) After we launched the name-calling insurance, Mike tried to collect when someone he didn't like (as opposed to a friend) called him "Sluggo." Ultimately, we ruled he couldn't collect—not because he hadn't been harmed, but because the policies were too vague.

We rewrote the policies to require purchasers to enumerate

the names they were protecting against. When people tried to get around that—say, by calling Mike "Slugmeister" instead of "Sluggo"—we added language covering "reasonable variations."

I don't remember if it helped curb the name calling. Probably not, but it was a lesson in communication and meaning, the consequences of choosing words when you need to be as precise as possible.

These sorts of experiences should not be impossible in today's classrooms, not as long as we return to teachers the freedom necessary to engage their students as teachers see fit. In fact, experiences like these are not only not impossible—there are thousands of teachers across America doing incredibly innovative work, even in the face of tight constraints.

The good news is that none of this has to be invented or built from scratch. The methods, philosophies, and resources are well established through organizations like the National Council of Teachers of English (NCTE), which offers a community for the sharing of ideas and provides materials and approaches to help support teaching writing in ways that extend beyond standardized assessments.

One of my most consistent frustrations with the systems in which we ask students to write is that we actually have a tremendous body of existing knowledge about what works and why it works.

One example of what works is something called "the writer's notebook," akin in some ways to Mrs. Minch's "12 Stories" portfolio. But the writer's notebook is even better, because it is used to record the process of writing as well as to memorialize the finished product. Filling the writer's notebook with the experiences that are then turned into writing reinforces writing as thinking, and feeling, and doing. The notebook is a tool of the writer's practice, and it can be incorporated into writing instruction as soon as children know how to write.[3]

Why am I less likely to remember my teachers the further along I progressed in my education? I can remember the names of exactly four of the thirty-five or so professors I had in college. My memories of class are nearly nonexistent.

But I can name every single one of my grade school teachers and can readily conjure memories from class from thirty-five to forty years ago. I remember learning. I remember being excited about learning, a feeling that gradually leeched away in each successive year of schooling and didn't return until I entered graduate school.

I don't believe this is just nostalgia. There was a difference in the quantity and quality of my work between when I was engaged—in grade school, and then again in graduate school—and when I was expected to keep marching up the educational ladder of "achievement."

Unfortunately, fewer and fewer students have the benefit of being allowed to explore their own minds, and are instead subjected to running the educational gauntlet, which requires them to sacrifice so much in the interests of "achievement." The damage we're doing has become apparent.

An approach that recognizes the humanity of each individual will help to mitigate this damage. Since we don't know who young writers are going to become, when they are writing we should let them be whoever they are.

What about the Teachers?

Teach Harder: Or Else

For years, teachers have been subjected to what Stanford professor of education Linda Darling-Hammond calls the "kick the dog harder model of education reform."[1]

There's a strain of the school reform movement that believes students will learn more if teachers learn to teach better—or not "better," but "harder." As Daniel Koretz of Harvard puts it, "The reformers' implicit assumption seemed to be that many teachers knew how to teach more effectively but were being withholding, and therefore confronting them with sanctions and rewards would be enough to get them to deliver."[2]

Policies that strip teachers of autonomy while tying their security to standardized test scores explicitly embrace this ethos, which leads to an atmosphere that is antithetical to learning. We should have been listening to teachers all along as they reported the damage being done to students.

In 2013, Kenneth Bernstein, a retired award-winning social studies teacher, wrote an open letter to college faculty. Published in the *Academe* blog of the American Association of University Professors, the letter offered "warnings from the trenches," telling faculty of what to expect from students entering their classrooms.[3]

Bernstein writes about his experience teaching AP US Government, preparing his students to do well on the exam (a professional responsibility) by teaching them "bad writing." He writes: "I would like to believe that I prepared them to think more critically and to present cogent arguments, but I could not simultaneously prepare them to do well on that portion of the test and teach them to write in a fashion that would properly serve them at higher levels of education."

Bernstein ends with a plea: "Please do not blame those of us in public schools for how unprepared for higher education the students arriving at your institutions are. We have very little say in what is happening to public education. Even the most distinguished and honored among us have trouble getting our voices heard in the discussion about educational policy."

It is hard to imagine another profession where its practitioners have less of a say in the specifics of their own work. The chief players and architects of school reform in the United States—Bill Gates, Arne Duncan, Betsy DeVos, David Coleman (the driving force behind the Common Core State Standards), and the countless think tank "wonks" churning out policy papers—have almost no experience working inside classrooms as teachers.

Thousands of teachers like Kenneth Bernstein who have witnessed the damage firsthand have been shouting from the rooftops but have been largely ignored.

These changes to education have been happening even as teaching has become an inherently more precarious and less attractive profession. Just as we've placed hurdles in front of students who are supposed to be learning writing, it would be hard to design a less effective system to help teachers perform their best.

Yes, there are bad teachers—just as there are bad doctors, bad lawyers, lousy actors, and washed-up ballplayers. There are also great teachers, good teachers, and average teachers. Nearly 100 percent of our efforts at teacher accountability are focused on identifying and removing the extremely small minority engaging in what we might consider professional malpractice. Rather than spending so much time, effort, and money to try to rank teachers as "good" or "bad," we should be focusing on teacher development, the same way we should be focusing on student development.

If we want teaching and teachers to improve, we should instead be creating a space where all teachers are given the freedom and resources to improve their practices. Kicking the dog has not worked. Dubious practices like Value Added Modeling (part of Koretz's "charade") will only serve to drive more and more teachers out of the profession.

Teaching is hard. It requires both disciplinary knowledge and experience to become competent, let alone good. For me, as a college instructor with a significant personal affinity for teaching, this evolution still took years, and it remains an ongoing process.

If we want to help teachers become better at teaching, we should first recognize that teaching is a profession with its own practice, and to improve at that practice teachers require what any professional needs: time, resources, and motivation.

Surveys show that most teachers enter the profession for altruistic reasons. Sixty-eight percent say they became a teacher to "make a difference in students' lives." Eighty-two percent say making a difference in students' lives is among the most rewarding aspects of teaching.[4]

These findings suggest that teachers are an extraordinarily motivated group, eager to pursue professional development and improve at their work. But we are crushing them under the weight of regulations and oversight. My home state of South Carolina is facing an "acute teacher shortage," with almost five thousand teachers leaving public schools in the 2016–2017 school year.[5]

One of those teachers, Jeremy Cantrill, from Cane Bay High School in Summerville, told a school board meeting in June 2017: "After four years, I no longer have the motivation or willpower to teach."

Cantrill was only twenty-nine years old when he left his job as a history teacher. He should have been entering his prime teaching years, but instead he "felt increasingly bogged down by competing state and district standards. He found himself spending a lot of time preparing students for an array of standardized tests when he would have rather been teaching material that interested them."[6]

He had become "a robot."

Jeremy Cantrill's story is playing out in thousands of classrooms across the country on a daily basis. Teacher after teacher will tell you it's not about the money, but the lack of autonomy and the pointless obstacles placed between them and their students.[7]

As we've seen in teacher uprisings in West Virginia, Oklahoma, and elsewhere, while improving compensation clearly matters to teachers, their primary goal is to secure the resources necessary to do their jobs well.

In the United States teachers spend too much of their workday in class, and their student loads are far too heavy to allow them the time necessary to engage in ongoing professional development.

Better teaching means putting teachers at the center of the teacher evaluation process, rather than relying on test scores with dubious relationships to learning, or even more dubious algorithms derived from those not-particularly-meaningful test scores. Early-career teachers should be consistently observed and evaluated by experienced teachers and administrators (who must be drawn from the teaching ranks). The focus should be on formative assessment, much as a football coaching staff will watch game film with a quarterback, dissecting what happened and looking for ways to improve next time out.

At the same time, teachers should be given significant time to engage in a reflective teaching practice through which they self-assess their work and seek out the counsel and collaboration of other educators through a continual process of improvement.

In many ways, this is already how well-functioning schools work. New hires seek out the old hands for wisdom. The trouble is, within our public school systems there's never enough time or resources to make this mentoring process anything more than catch-as-catch-can. If these responsibilities could be formalized, reducing course loads for experienced teachers who are engaging in mentorship while keeping student loads low for newer teachers, every school could become a learning community. This atmosphere already exists at elite schools such as Lakeside Prep in Seattle, where Bill Gates's children were educated, or Sidwell Friends in Washington, DC, where President Obama's daughters attended.

Inside these communities, when schools are working well, the average become good, the good great, the great tremendous. When a truly incompetent or malevolent person is identified, the community has a mechanism to remove them, because communities where values are widely shared are adept at self-policing. Instead of allowing public schools agency over their own cultures and practices, we police them from on high with ill-considered "accountability" regimes. What works in elite institutions will work in public ones, provided sufficient resources are available to build those positive community practices.

All teachers should be given resources to attend professional conferences and engage in continuing education. Too many of the helpful resources made available by groups like the NCTE are locked away, not because teachers don't want them, but because they do not have the time to access and work with them. Too many teachers are just trying to survive day to day. We know a lot about how best to teach writing. We now need the will to put that knowledge to work.

When I describe these philosophies as a superior alternative to our current system of accountability, sometimes people will say something like, "Man, you sure do put a lot of trust in people."

In fact, the opposite is true. I am suspicious of people, including myself, especially when we are alone or atomized, rather than joined together in compounds. I can be as lazy as anyone, but it is considerably easier to be less lazy when I know others—such as students—are relying on me to do my part.

Knowing there are others on whom I can rely when I am not at my best also helps me soldier through those moments. I believe we are smarter and wiser when working collectively than when alone.

Regarding the teaching of writing specifically, I believe teachers should assume additional responsibilities.

If we are truly going to value writing, teaching writing must extend beyond English or Language Arts classes. A framework that uses the writer's practice and experiences rather than prescriptive assignments is adaptable to any discipline. Writing as thinking is not confined to a single subject; it's merely a matter of considering the kind of thinking we would like students to practice in different disciplines, and then designing experiences around them.

My first encounter with writing experiences came long before I even considered such a framework, when I attended a conference at Virginia Tech on the topic of writing across the curriculum. We were tasked with developing new approaches. One of the members of my group, an art history professor, had tired of giving what she called "name, date, period, significance" exams, in which students simply regurgitated information. Reconsidering what she wanted students to learn, she transformed the test into an assignment where the students were to act as curators for a museum, selecting paintings and arranging them spatially in an exhibit. They would write descriptions of the paintings on the walls of their exhibit, and they would write a separate short piece describing the rationale for how the paintings were chosen and arranged.

It was a brilliant idea, and years later the concept came back to me as I was rethinking my own assignments.

I also believe writing teachers should be writers. I don't mean they must be professional writers, or even seek publication for their writing, but as part of their educational community they should at least be asked to reflect upon and write about their teaching. The same metacognitive reflective process we engage with students should apply to teachers as well.

If we treat teachers like the professionals they are, and if we give them the necessary time and space to act as professionals, we will see continuous improvement.

Certainly the policies we've been pursuing for the last thirty years are not working: they have served primarily to make teaching a less and less attractive profession, while driving teachers out of the ranks at an alarming pace.

At this point, what do we have to lose by empowering teachers to act as the professionals they are?

Helping the Permanent Higher Education Underclass

At the college level, the story of those who shoulder most of the burden of teaching writing is more one of neglect than the outright mistreatment we see in the K–12 sector. The economic, cultural, and political forces that have resulted in the widespread casualization of the laborers who do most of the teaching of writing in college would take another book to dissect.

Remedying the distorted labor structures of higher education will take truly revolutionary steps, but every day we fail to address the problem we are one step closer to collapse.

We could argue that writing as a discipline should be divorced from English. Why writing is housed in the English department is an accident of history, an artifact from when English meant English literature. Once writing became a discipline unto itself, it fell to English because . . . well . . . because. As institutions have evolved, first-year writing (composition) has become, in many cases, its own entity, if not separate in terms of administrative structure, often taught by faculty who are not afforded the same pay, status, or security as others.

Contingent teachers of first-year writing have become a kind of permanent underclass at many institutions. Even at institutions where first-year writing isn't staffed largely by contingent faculty, student loads are often too high and resources too limited. First-year writing is in theory an important class nearly every student takes, and yet it is almost entirely neglected by anyone above the department level, and in many cases is neglected even at the department level.

Whatever the causes, we are stuck with the reality. The consequences of the status quo have been clear for a generation or more, and yet only limited progress has been made.

Rather than opening much larger debates about tenure or tuition or status, I believe we should start with a set of goals for those who teach writing. We know the conditions effective teaching requires, and we should seek to meet them:

1. Course and student loads need to be brought into line with disciplinary recommendations: no more than three sections per instructor per semester, totaling no more than sixty students.
2. Instructors should have the opportunity to participate in all relevant departmental governance, most specifically including decision making over course curriculum.
3. Instructors must have access to all necessary resources for teaching, including office space, library resources, sufficient classroom space, and computers/networks.
4. Instructors should be paid a per-course salary equivalent to the compensation earned by full-time/tenure-track faculty at the same institution doing similar work. The Modern Language Association recommends $10,700 per 3-hour course—more than three times the current average per-course compensation.[8]
5. Any instructor working full-time-equivalent hours should be eligible for health and other employment benefits.

People who work inside higher education institutions will tell me how impossible all of this is. Over $10,000 per class will seem like a fantasy, even though it would result in salaries of only around $60,000 a year for people with advanced degrees who are teaching college full-time. People will say it's too costly. We'll have to hire more people and pay everyone more to boot. Where will the money come from?

It's a big question, and a big problem. I wish I had an answer. Clearly it involves taking money that currently goes to something else and putting it into education. As I write this, the United States is collectively wealthier than at any other time in its existence. And tomorrow it will be wealthier still.

We may lack the will. Or we may lack the ability to agree on what deserves attention and funding.

But we don't lack for money, that's for sure.

In Conclusion

A Beautiful Dream

Here is my dream vision for the future:

A powerful/wealthy/influential figure inside the education movement—possibly Bill Gates or Mark Zuckerberg, or maybe an amalgam of both we'll call "Zuckergates"—reads this book, the scales fall from Zuckergates's eyes as the sheer brilliance of my ideas bores into Zuckergates's brain, after which Zuckergates abandons all other charitable endeavors and dedicates every ounce of their energy and fortune to making sure my approaches to teaching writing are adopted in every classroom across the country.

Problem solved.

Except not.

Billionaires like Gates and Zuckerberg have been shoveling money at education with demonstrably negative effects, often backing "solutions" (such as Gates's championing of the Common Core State Standards) that leave teachers, students, and communities behind. There is no quick fix for improving education.

Addressing Reality

Teaching and learning is complicated, context-dependent, and incredibly variable from one situation to another. I have taught exactly the same course material to nearly identical sets of students in back-to-back class periods and have had remarkably different experiences.

We have misplaced our faith in fads that promise solutions, because to contemplate a world without solutions is too difficult to confront. We have attempted to systematize things (like learning) that are not systematic. We have neglected the human capital—the people who engage in the actual work of teaching.

The evidence is overwhelming that we have been wrong in the way we teach students to write and think, but we shouldn't fall prey to thinking a simple course correction will lead to a solution. That mentality is what got us into this situation in the first place.

Learning to write is a process, not a product. There is no finish line, only the ongoing work to keep developing the writer's practice. I shared the frameworks I discuss in this book because I believe they can be helpful, but a framework is exactly that—a scaffold on which to build other structures, some of which may look radically different from each other.

Rather than concerning ourselves with techniques or "best practices," which are pitched as universally employable, the process should be focused at the student/teacher level. The first step is to create the conditions under which learning is most likely to happen. This can be achieved through collaboration between students and teachers (and, where appropriate, parents and administrators), but I believe first we must do better at listening to students who are telling us what they need in order to thrive.

The rates of anxiety and depression, the expressions of a love of learning (but hating school), the open longing for a time when they can get off the treadmill and actually live lives oriented around their desires, all demonstrate a world where students are not being heard, not being respected.

Similarly, we must do significantly better to support teachers and give them the necessary freedom to do their work well. This not only means freedom to teach in ways that best meet their students' needs, but also ensuring reasonable workloads coupled with sufficient economic security, which will allow teachers to dedicate themselves to this process.

This book questions and confronts the values that underpin some of the historical and contemporary approaches to how we educate students. *A Nation at Risk*, No Child Left Behind, Race to the Top, Common Core State Standards—for much of the last thirty-plus years we have been seeking a top-down solution where the "best" approach can be imposed and adopted nationwide.

As wonderful as it may seem, and as lucrative as it would be to have this book and my philosophies adopted by Zuckergates, this is not a productive way forward.

Change must happen at the grassroots level, as individuals are given the time and space necessary to question what's been done in the past and develop approaches consistent with their values and student needs and experiences going forward. Change will be slow and fitful, and it will be difficult to measure the impacts through quantification, but this is part of the point.

There will be no single measurement to tell us what's "working." We will know it is working if we are doing the work.

Process, not product. I believe root-level change works because I've lived it. Discontented by what I and my students were experiencing, I began to question the ways of teaching that had been handed down to me. To arrive at the ideas and approaches in this book required iteration after iteration. While I believe the frameworks I propose could help shorten the learning curve for others, all changes will take time, and they will include periods that feel like setbacks, because that's exactly what they are.

My story, as an under-the-radar contingent college instructor, has been unusual. I enjoyed extraordinary freedom because the system generally doesn't care enough about people in my position to spend time monitoring what we're up to. At the same time, because of fortunate circumstances, I was not overly concerned about holding on to my job, and that freedom allowed me to experiment and innovate.

Freedom's just another word for nothing left to lose. Leaving teachers alone would be a significant improvement over the ways we box them around from reform to reform, expecting sudden miracles without giving them the resources to fashion these wonders.

I experienced a kind of benign neglect, which allowed me to develop as an instructor, but we can't expect similar conditions to be useful on a larger scale.

The role of governments, school administrations, and parents should be to help set the values we would like to see enacted, and then help ensure the conditions at the school and class level that allow for those values to be practiced. This is not a utopian idea, impossible to implement. It simply means having a deeper discussion about what it means for students to "learn" (a discussion we've pushed off for far too long) and to then support the experts, teachers and students, as they pursue the work that fosters learning.

Yes, the experts about what happens during the learning process are teachers and students, and we should be listening to them as they express what they need in order to thrive. We should strive for communities where students and teachers can experience what psychologists call "belongingness."[1] Students who feel "accepted" and empowered, who are given a voice in their community that is heard and respected, are more engaged with school, more committed to learning, and more giving of themselves to those they are surrounded by. This should be the goal of education. Generations of students have been subjected to something close to the opposite, a competition rather than a collaboration, and the effects couldn't be clearer in their attitudes toward schooling and even toward the world beyond.

Teachers and students have been letting us know both implicitly and explicitly for years that we've been off track, but they have been largely ignored. It's time not only to listen to them, but to put them at the center of the discussions. We must shift away from "solutions" brought to us by philanthropists, think tanks, politicians, economists, psychologists, and now even neuroscientists, and instead consider the specific cultures in which education happens. As we act within those cultures and conditions change, creating new cultures, we must reflect and alter course as necessary.

Process, not product.

We must listen to the educators and those being educated while recognizing that each of us falls into both of those categories simultaneously.

Let the conversations begin.

Acknowledgments

I've had a very unusual "career" as an instructor and "academic," which is why those two words appear in quotes. I have taught at four different institutions without ever being on the tenure track, and the focus of my work has sometimes been markedly different from one stop to the next. While my unconventional path has prevented me from achieving status or security inside the academy, in many ways my being "contingent," with no motive other than to improve my craft for its own sake, has led to the writing of this book. Had I followed a more conventional path, seeking a tenured position in creative writing (my terminal degree), it seems doubtful, whether I ever achieved that goal, that I would have become interested in issues of writing pedagogy, and certainly not to the point that I'd write a book like this one.

In a lot of ways I've lived an ideal life as an academic, free to pursue a variety of interests while publishing in different disciplines and genres. I was allowed to do this, however, only because I was not subject to the accountability and strictures that attach to one's pursuit of tenure. Consider the irony: I've been able to assemble the CV of a senior scholar with a public profile because I never pursued the institutional status of a senior scholar with a public profile. The downside is that I was paid between one-third and one-half the salary I would have received as tenurable faculty, and the opportunity cost of teaching as a part-time adjunct is too high to justify. In this case, my fate is similar to far too many contingent college faculty. The number of dedicated and talented people I have seen flushed out of education is mind-boggling. It is an unconscionable waste.

During my journeys, I've been extraordinarily fortunate to encounter people willing to support and invest in me and my work, and people who have significantly influenced the contents of this book.

In addition, the miracle of online and social spaces has introduced me to a community of writers and teachers who share and explore many of the concerns I grapple with in this book. Online, my contingent status is irrelevant, as I've been allowed and encouraged to engage with and learn from this group of dedicated professionals. I cite work from many of them in this book, but they deserve a separate acknowledgment here.

I wish I could tell the world in detail how and why each of these people has been influential, but there just isn't space, so I'm listing them here instead: John Wood, Nick Johnson, Neil Connelly, Adam Johnson, Philip Graham, John Griswold, Marlene Preston, Susanna Ashton, Keith Morris, Will Gray, Bill Stanton, Chris Warnick, Myra Seaman, Conseula Francis, Scott Peeples, Anna Lonon, Paula Patch, Paul Thomas, James Lang, Joshua Eyler, Lee Skallerup Bessette, Susan Schorn, Susan Blum, Barbara Fister, Cathy Davidson, Jesse Stommel, Daniel Chambliss, Audrey Watters, Kelly Baker, Sherri Spelic, Jacinta Yanders, Catherine Prendergast, Tressie McMillan Cottom, Sara Goldrick-Rab, Robin DeRosa, David Perry, Jon Becker, Bonni Stachowiak, Sarah Rose Cavanagh, Kevin Gannon, Peter Greene.

A separate thanks goes to Doug Lederman and Scott Jaschik, of *Inside Higher Ed,* who have consistently supported this work by providing me a platform at their website. When I write about the conditions under which we do our best work, having a place where you are heard and respected is high on the list, and Doug and Scott run *IHE* with incredible energy and integrity.

Thanks also to Greg Britton, Catherine Goldstead, Hilary S. Jacqmin, and everyone else at Johns Hopkins University Press. Greg was especially encouraging with his belief that what I'd been blogging about could become a book. The care Catherine and Hilary have taken with steering the project through the publishing process and production of the manuscript itself is beyond compare.

Thank you to David Goehring for his patient and expert copyediting work. He has saved me from broadcasting many mistakes, and any errors in the text are definitely my fault.

Thank you to Mel Flashman at Janklow & Nesbit for her expert and caring guidance.

And thank you to my family, who has supported me always, and especially to my wife, Kathy: I'll follow you wherever you go.

Notes

· ·

Our Writing "Crisis"

1. "Balance Bikes Overtake Training Wheels for Young Riders," *NBC News*, October 2, 2015. https://www.nbcnews.com/business/consumer /balance-bikes-overtake-training-wheels-teaching-young-riders -n436971.

2. And yet, interestingly, much of what I have to say is well known among teachers of writing and those who study rhetoric and composition. One of the recurring themes of this book will be how much we know but don't actually do to address the teaching of writing.

Johnny Could Never Write

1. Adams Sherman Hill, "An Answer to the Cry for More English," *Twenty Years of School and College English* (Harvard University, 1896), 6.

2. For more detailed coverage see Ronald T. Kellogg, "Training Writing Skills: A Cognitive Developmental Perspective," *Journal of Writing Research* (2008): 2–23.

3. Helen Sword, "How Academics Survive the Writing Grind: Some Anecdotal Advice," *Literary Hub,* September 7, 2017. http://lithub.com /how-academics-survive-the-writing-grind-some-anecdotal-advice/.

4. It's titled "The Monkey Sidekick: Stories," and the only remaining copies are in my living room and the library at McNeese State University in Lake Charles, Louisiana—at least until I figure out how to break in and destroy the evidence.

5. Helen Sword, *Air & Light & Time & Space: How Successful Academics Write* (Cambridge, MA: Harvard University Press, 2017).

6. Anne Trubek, "Student Writing in the Digital Age," *JSTOR Daily*, October 19, 2016. https://daily.jstor.org/student-writing-in-the-digital -age/.

7. Andrea A. Lunsford and Karen J. Lunsford, "Mistakes Are a Fact of Life: A National Comparative Study," *College Composition and Communication* 59, no. 4 (June 2008): 795–796.

8. Quoted in Matt Richtel, "Blogs vs. Term Papers," *New York Times*, January 20, 2012. http://www.nytimes.com/2012/01/22/education

/edlife/muscling-in-on-the-term-paper-tradition.html?partner
=rss&emc=rss%C2%A0%C2%A0%C2%A0%C2%A0.

The Writer's Practice

1. In fact, this chapter on the writer's practice was moved several times during the drafting of this book. It was initially the second chapter, but I moved it to where it sits presently, and then I moved it again to part 2 of the book before returning it to this spot. I'm confident I will pick up a finished copy of this book and wonder if I still should have put it somewhere else. Part of the writer's practice is knowing that being "finished" with a project is an illusion. At some point, circumstances simply force you to stop.

2. The concept of the writer's practice was not even part of the initial outline submitted to the publisher when the project was accepted. Only once I started drafting from the outline did it occur to me that I needed to discuss this material.

3. I had never even heard of this term until I googled "systems of the body." It involves the skin, hair, nails, and sweat.

4. Council of Writing Program Administrators, National Council of Teachers of English, National Writing Project, "Framework for Success in Postsecondary Writing," January 2011. http://wpacouncil.org/framework.

The Five-Paragraph Essay

1. James T. Davis II, "Two New Heuristics in Response to Formulaic Writing: What Lies beyond Oversimplified Composition Instruction" (PhD dissertation, Georgia State University, 2011), 62–65.

2. As quoted in Tina Nazerian, "Is the Five-Paragraph Essay Dead?" *EdSurge*, October 18, 2017. https://www.edsurge.com/news/2017-10-18-is-the-five-paragraph-essay-dead.

The Problem of Atmosphere

1. I have been doing this experiment for over fifteen years at three different institutions (Virginia Tech, Clemson, College of Charleston), and the percentage of students who would take the deal has steadily increased from around 40 percent when I started to the 80–85 percent range today.

2. Gallup, 2016 Gallup Student Poll Snapshot Report. http://news.gallup.com/reports/210995/6.aspx?utm_source=link_studentpoll2&utm_campaign=item_188039&utm_medium=copy. Student engagement ticks up very slightly in twelfth grade as students see the light at

the end of the tunnel, but it is still well below that of fifth graders, or any grade other than eleventh.

3. Isabella Bruyere, "Why School Sucks (Hint: It's Not Because It's 'Boring')," *Medium*, July 13, 2017. https://medium.com/@BellaBruyere /why-school-sucks-hint-its-not-because-it-s-boring-221cc1a67576.

4. Susan D. Blum, *"I Love Learning; I Hate School": An Anthropology of College* (Ithaca, NY: Cornell University Press, 2016), 7.

5. Blum, 3.

6. To preserve as much student anonymity as possible in the personal examples and illustrations, "they" is used as a non-gendered pronoun throughout the book.

7. Alexander W. Astin, Kenneth C. Green, William S. Korn, and Marilynn Schalit, *The American Freshman: National Norms for Fall 1985* (Los Angeles: Cooperative Institutional Research Program at the Higher Education Research Institute [HERI], UCLA, 1986), https://www.heri .ucla.edu/PDFs/pubs/TFS/Norms/Monographs/TheAmericanFresh- man1985.pdf; John H. Pryor, Kevin Eagan, Laura Palucki Blake, Sylvia Hurtado, Jennifer Berdan, and Matthew H. Case, *The American Fresh- man: National Norms Fall 2012* (Los Angeles: Cooperative Institutional Research Program at the Higher Education Research Institute [HERI], UCLA, 2013), https://www.heri.ucla.edu/monographs/TheAmerican Freshman2012.pdf; Kevin Eagan, Ellen Bara Stolzenberg, Hilary B. Zimmerman, Melissa C. Aragon, Hannah Whang Sayson, and Cecilia Rios-Aguilar, *The American Freshman: National Norms Fall 2016* (Los Angeles: Cooperative Institutional Research Program at the Higher Education Research Institute [HERI], UCLA, 2017). https://www.heri .ucla.edu/monographs/TheAmericanFreshman2016.pdf.

8. Ramin Mojtabai, Mark Olfson, and Beth Han, "National Trends in the Prevalence and Treatment of Depression in Adolescents and Young Adults," *Pediatrics*, November 2016, http://pediatrics.aappublications.org /content/early/2016/11/10/peds.2016-1878; "More Stress, Less Stigma Drives College Students to Mental Health Services," *PBS NewsHour*, September 2, 2015. https://www.pbs.org/newshour/show/mental-health.

9. American College Health Association, "American College Health Association—National College Health Assessment II: Under- graduate Students Only, Reference Group Executive Summary, Fall 2011" (Hanover, MD: American College Health Association, 2012), 14, http://www.acha-ncha.org/docs/ACHA-NCHA-II_UNDERGRAD _ReferenceGroup_ExecutiveSummary_Fall2011.pdf; American College Health Association, "American College Health Association—National College Health Assessment II: Undergraduate Students Only, Reference

Group Executive Summary, Fall 2016" (Hanover, MD: American College Health Association, 2017), 14. http://www.acha-ncha.org/docs/NCHA-II_FALL_2016_UNDERGRADUATE_REFERENCE_GROUP_EXECUTIVE_SUMMARY.pdf.

10. Yanan Wang, "CDC Investigates Why So Many Students in Wealthy Palo Alto, Calif., Commit Suicide," *Washington Post*, February 16, 2016. https://www.washingtonpost.com/news/morning-mix/wp/2016/02/16/cdc-investigates-why-so-many-high-school-students-in-wealthy-palo-alto-have-committed-suicide/?utm_term=.1ee0ec51453e.

11. Scott Jaschik, "Suicide Note Calls Out Pressure on Students," *Inside Higher Ed*, February 12, 2018. https://www.insidehighered.com/admissions/article/2018/02/12/suicide-note-16-year-old-renews-debate-about-pressure-top-high-schools.

The Problem of Surveillance

1. Aaron E. Carroll, "Wearable Fitness Devices Don't Seem to Make You Fitter," *New York Times*, February 20, 2017. https://www.nytimes.com/2017/02/20/upshot/wearable-fitness-devices-dont-seem-to-make-you-more-fit.html?mcubz=3&_r=0.

2. Audrey Watters, "The History of the Pedometer (and the Problems with Learning Analytics)," *Hack Education*, June 22, 2017. http://hackeducation.com/2017/06/22/fitbit.

3. Natasha Singer, "Teacher's New Pet: An App That Tracks Students," *New York Times*, November 19, 2014. https://www.nytimes.com/times-insider/2014/11/19/teachers-new-pet-an-app-that-tracks-students/?mcubz=3&_r=0.

4. Natasha Singer, "Privacy Concerns for ClassDojo and Other Tracking Apps for Schoolchildren," *New York Times*, November 16, 2014. https://www.nytimes.com/2014/11/17/technology/privacy-concerns-for-classdojo-and-other-tracking-apps-for-schoolchildren.html.

5. As we imagine the depth and breadth of the data that will be aggregated by these apps, we also should be concerned about the potential for that data to be stolen or misused. This is not a theoretical concern. Doug Levin, an independent education technology consultant, tracks what he calls "K–12 cyber incidents," which include phishing attacks resulting in disclosure of personal data, ransomware attacks, and other incidents that put student data and privacy at risk. Between January 2016 (when the list was started) and April 8, 2018 (the most recent date for which data was available before this book went to press), Levin identified 323 incidents, almost surely an undercount, as many incidents are not publicly known or shared. Levin's website will provide the most

current tally: https://www.edtechstrategies.com/k-12-cyber-incident-map/.

6. Jessica Lahey, *The Gift of Failure: How the Best Parents Learn to Let Go So Their Children Can Succeed* (New York: HarperCollins, 2015).

7. Amar Toor, "This French School Is Using Facial Recognition to Find Out When Students Aren't Paying Attention," *The Verge*, May 26, 2017. https://www.theverge.com/2017/5/26/15679806/ai-education-facial-recognition-nestor-france.

8. Sydney Johnson, "This Company Wants to Gather Student Brainwave Data to Measure 'Engagement,'" *EdSurge*, October 26, 2017. https://www.edsurge.com/news/2017-10-26-this-company-wants-to-gather-student-brainwave-data-to-measure-engagement.

9. Darryl Robinson, "I Went to Some of D.C.'s Best Schools. I Was Still Unprepared for College," *Washington Post*, April 13, 2012. https://www.washingtonpost.com/opinions/i-went-to-one-of-dcs-best-high-schools-i-was-still-unprepared-for-college/2012/04/13/gIQAqQQAFT_story.html?utm_term=.402603afeb1f.

10. Joanne W. Golann, "The Paradox of Success at a No-Excuses School," *Sociology of Education* 88, no. 2 (January 14, 2015): 108.

11. Caroline Williams, "How to Daydream Your Way to Better Learning and Concentration," *New Scientist*, May 17, 2017, https://www.newscientist.com/article/mg23431260-200-how-to-daydream-your-way-to-better-learning-and-concentration/; Katrina Schwartz, "Why Daydreaming Is Critical to Effective Learning," *MindShift*, October 6, 2014. https://ww2.kqed.org/mindshift/2014/10/06/why-daydreaming-is-critical-to-effective-learning/.

The Problem of Assessment and Standardization

1. The National Commission on Excellence in Education, *A Nation at Risk: The Imperative for Educational Reform*, 1983. https://www.edreform.com/wp-content/uploads/2013/02/A_Nation_At_Risk_1983.pdf.

2. Dana Goldstein, "The Schoolmaster," *The Atlantic*, October 2012. https://www.theatlantic.com/magazine/archive/2012/10/the-schoolmaster/309091/.

3. Daniel Koretz, *The Testing Charade: Pretending to Make Schools Better* (Chicago: University of Chicago Press, 2017), 1.

4. Rick Hess, "Has K–12 Education Fallen for a Testing Charade?" *Education Week*, September 28, 2017. http://blogs.edweek.org/edweek/rick_hess_straight_up/2017/09/5_thoughts_on_dan_koretzs_the_testing_charade.html?platform=hootsuite.

5. Robert Pondiscio, "Education Reform Is Off Track. Here's How to Fix It," *Flypaper* (Thomas B. Fordham Institute, January 24, 2018). https://edexcellence.net/articles/education-reform-is-off-track-heres-how-to-fix-it.

6. Shankar Vedantam, "Examining Links between Academic Performance and Food Stamps," *Morning Edition*, NPR, September 21, 2017. https://www.npr.org/2017/09/21/552530614/researchers-examine-links-between-academic-performance-and-food-stamps.

7. Zachary A. Goldfarb, "These Four Charts Show How the SAT Favors Rich, Educated Families," *Washington Post*, March 5, 2014. https://www.washingtonpost.com/news/wonk/wp/2014/03/05/these-four-charts-show-how-the-sat-favors-the-rich-educated-families/?utm_term=.3160b7278925.

8. Paul Thomas, "What's Responsible for America's Persistent Achievement Gap?" *Alternet*, February 3, 2015. https://www.alternet.org/education/central-issue-heart-americas-growing-education-gap.

9. Sean F. Reardon, "The Widening Academic Achievement Gap between the Rich and the Poor," in *Whither Opportunity? Rising Inequality and the Uncertain Life Chance of Low-Income Children* (New York: Russell Sage Foundation Press, 2011).

10. Andrea Gabor, "The Myth of the New Orleans Miracle School Makeover," *New York Times*, August 22, 2015. https://www.nytimes.com/2015/08/23/opinion/sunday/the-myth-of-the-new-orleans-school-makeover.html.

11. Mark Niesse, "Charges Expected in APS Test-Cheating Scandal," *Atlanta Journal-Constitution*, March 25, 2013, http://www.ajc.com/news/local/charges-expected-aps-test-cheating-scandal/d2whbQMFan5rbWgTHbSFsO/; Rachel Aviv, "Wrong Answer," *New Yorker*, July 21, 2014, https://www.newyorker.com/magazine/2014/07/21/wrong-answer; John Merrow, "Michelle Rhee's Reign of Error," *Learning Matters*, April 11, 2013, https://themerrowreport.com/2017/11/11/the-d-c-school-reform-fiasco-a-complete-history/; Greg Toppo, "Memo Warns of Rampant Cheating in D.C. Public Schools," *USA Today*, April 11, 2013, https://www.usatoday.com/story/news/nation/2013/04/11/memo-washington-dc-schools-cheating/2074473/.

The legacy of the earlier cheating scandal under chancellor Michelle Rhee that arose out of Rhee's punitive policies toward teachers has resurfaced in the 2017 news of Ballou High School. Once championed as the place where every student went to college, Ballou in reality suffered from chronic absenteeism, which was overlooked and ignored in order to fuel a narrative of successful school reform. Kate McGee, "What Really Happened at the School Where Every Graduate Got into College," *All Things Considered*, November 28, 1027; Peter Jamison and Fenit Nirappil, "Once a National Model, Now D.C. Public Schools Target of FBI Investigation," *Washington Post*, February 2, 2018.

12. Christopher Tienken, "Students' Test Scores Tell Us More about the Community They Live in Than What They Know," *The Conversation*, July 5, 2017. https://theconversation.com/students-test-scores-tell-us-more-about-the-community-they-live-in-than-what-they-know-77934.

13. Harkius, customer review of *The Funny Man*, Amazon.com, October 20, 2011. https://www.amazon.com/Funny-Man-John-Warner/product-reviews/1569479739/ref=cm_cr_dp_d_ttl?ie=UTF8&reviewerType=all_reviews&sortBy=recent#R5MMHIGXU8QH5.

14. John Warner, *The Funny Man* (New York: Soho Press, 2011).

15. William Faulkner, Goodreads.com. https://www.goodreads.com/quotes/320275I-a-hack-writer-who-would-not-have-been-considered-fourth.

16. "October 2014—SAT Essay Prompts," CrackSat.net. http://www.cracksat.net/sat/essay/156.html#ufKZOJLOogJrtXWT.99.

17. Matthew J. X. Malady, "We Are Teaching High School Students to Write Terribly," *Slate*, October 10, 2013. http://www.slate.com/articles/life/education/2013/10/sat_essay_section_problems_with_grading_instruction_and_prompts.html.

18. Nick Anderson, "'Read Me!': Students Race to Craft Forceful College Essays as Deadlines Near," *Washington Post*, October 28, 2017. https://www.washingtonpost.com/local/education/read-me-students-race-to-craft-forceful-college-essays-as-deadlines-near/2017/10/28/0384fcae-b808-11e7-be94-fabb0f1e9ffb_story.html?utm_term=.3a4b366f895e.

19. Arthur Applebee and Judith Langer, "A Snapshot of Writing Instruction in Middle Schools and High Schools," *English Journal* 100.6 (2011): 14–27.

20. Charles Sampson, "As a Superintendent, I Am Gravely Concerned. As a Parent, I Am Outraged," *Washington Post*, December 8, 2017. https://www.washingtonpost.com/news/answer-sheet/wp/2017/12/08/as-a-superintendent-i-am-gravely-concerned-as-a-parent-i-am-outraged/?

21. Anya Kamenetz, "Testing: How Much Is Too Much?" *NPR Ed*, November 17, 2014. https://www.npr.org/sections/ed/2014/11/17/362339421/testing-how-much-is-too-much.

The Problem of Education Fads

1. Walter Mischel and Ebbe B. Ebbesen, "Attention in Delay of Gratification," *Journal of Personality and Social Psychology* 16, no. 2 (October 1970), 329–337.

2. Walter Mischel, *The Marshmallow Test: Mastering Self-Control* (New York: Little, Brown, 2014).

3. Celeste Kidd, Holly Palmeri, and Richard N. Aslin, "Rational Snacking: Young Children's Decision-Making on the Marshmallow Task Is Moderated by Beliefs about Environmental Reliability," *Cognition* 126, no. 1 (January 2013): 109–114.

4. Michaeleen Doucleff, "Want to Teach Your Kids Self-Control? Ask a Cameroonian Farmer," *Morning Edition,* NPR, July 3, 2017. https://www.npr.org/sections/goatsandsoda/2017/07/03/534743719/want-to-teach-your-kids-self-control-ask-a-cameroonian-farmer.

5. Not enough to not title his own book *The Marshmallow Test*, but it's important to see that researchers who provide the origins for ideas that become education fads later come to regret or even renounce their work as it has been applied in education. This is a pattern we'll see throughout this chapter.

6. Jacoba Urist, "What the Marshmallow Test Really Teaches about Self Control," *The Atlantic*, September 24, 2014. https://www.theatlantic.com/health/archive/2014/09/what-the-marshmallow-test-really-teaches-about-self-control/380673/.

7. Nancy Chick, "Learning Styles," *Vanderbilt Center for Teaching*. https://cft.vanderbilt.edu/guides-sub-pages/learning-styles-preferences/.

8. Alfie Kohn, *Punished by Rewards: The Trouble with Gold Stars, Incentive Plans, A's, Praise, and Other Bribes* (Boston, MA: Houghton Mifflin Harcourt, 1993).

9. Daniel Pink, *Drive: The Surprising Truth about What Motivates Us* (New York: Riverhead, 2009).

10. Kaitlin Woolley and Ayelet Fishbach, "Immediate Rewards Predict Adherence to Long-Term Goals," *Personal and Social Psychology Bulletin* 43, no. 2 (February 2017): 151–162. https://www.ncbi.nlm.nih.gov/pubmed/27899467.

11. Nick Tasler, "The Marshmallow Myth," *Psychology Today*, March 9, 2017. https://www.psychologytoday.com/blog/strategic-thinking/201703/the-marshmallow-myth. (Italics in the original.)

12. Angela Duckworth, "Grit: The Power of Passion and Perseverance," TED Talks Education, April 2013. https://www.ted.com/talks/angela_lee_duckworth_grit_the_power_of_passion_and_perseverance.

13. Paul Tough, *How Children Succeed: Grit, Curiosity, and the Hidden Power of Character* (Boston, MA: Houghton Mifflin Harcourt, 2012).

14. KIPP, "Focus on Character." Accessed February 11, 2017. http://www.kipp.org/approach/character/.

15. Jeffrey Aaron Snyder, "Teaching Kids 'Grit' Is All the Rage. Here's What's Wrong with It," *New Republic*, May 6, 2014. https://newrepublic.com/article/117615/problem-grit-kipp-and-character-based-education.

16. Kate Zernike, "Testing for Joy and Grit? Schools Nationwide Push to Measure Students' Emotional Skills," *New York Times*, February 29, 2016. https://www.nytimes.com/2016/03/01/us/testing-for-joy-and-grit-schools-nationwide-push-to-measure-students-emotional-skills.html?_r=0.

17. Zernike.

18. Snyder.

19. Angela Duckworth, *Grit: The Power of Passion and Perseverance* (New York: Scribner, 2016), 46.

20. Dan Kois, "Why Do Writers Abandon Novels?" *New York Times*, March 4, 2011. https://www.nytimes.com/2011/03/06/books/review/Kois-t.html.

21. Rotten Tomatoes. Accessed February 11, 2018. https://www.rottentomatoes.com/m/after_earth/.

22. Alfie Kohn, "'Grit' Part 2—Is 'Slack' What Kids Need?" *SpeEd Change*, January 23, 2014. http://speedchange.blogspot.com/2014/01/grit-part-2-is-slack-what-kids-need.html.

23. Paul Tough, *Helping Children Succeed* (Boston, MA: Houghton Mifflin Harcourt, 2016).

24. UPI, "Study Ties I.Q. Scores to Stress," *New York Times*, May 31, 1983, http://www.nytimes.com/1983/05/31/science/study-ties-iq-scores-to-stress.html; United Sates Department of Agriculture, "The National School Lunch Program," accessed February 11, 2018, https://fns-prod.azureedge.net/sites/default/files/cn/NSLPFactSheet.pdf; Ernesto Pollitt, "Nutrition and Educational Achievement," 1984. https://eric.ed.gov/?id=ED254496.

25. Linda F. Nathan, *When Grit Isn't Enough: A High School Principal Examines How Poverty and Inequality Thwart the College-for-All Promise* (Boston, MA: Beacon Press, 2017).

The Problem of Technology Hype

1. Thomas Edison. https://quoteinvestigator.com/2012/02/15/books-obsolete/.

2. Audrey Watters, "Education Technology and Skinner's Box," *Hack Education*, February 10, 2015. http://hackeducation.com/2015/02/10/skinners-box.

3. Steven Leckart, "The Stanford Education Experiment Could Change Higher Learning Forever," *Wired*, March 20, 2012. https://www.wired.com/2012/03/ff_aiclass/. One of the features of hype in education technology is how often these claims ("change higher learning forever") show up in tech publications by people without the experience or expertise to make the claims. Of course, this is a feature of tech journalism in general, where the next revolution is always just around the corner, but it seems particularly pronounced when tech writers write about education.

4. Clarissa Shen, "Sebastian Thrun Wins Smithsonian American Ingenuity Award in Education for Udacity Work!" *Udacity* (blog), November 26, 2012. https://blog.udacity.com/2012/11/sebastian-thrun-wins-smithsonian.html.

5. Max Chafkin, "Udacity's Sebastian Thrun, Godfather of Free Online Education, Changes Course," *Fast Company*, November 14, 2013. https://www.fastcompany.com/3021473/udacity-sebastian-thrun-uphill-climb.

6. Jeffrey R. Young, "Udacity Official Declares MOOCs 'Dead' (Though the Company Still Offers Them)," *EdSurge*, October 12, 2017. https://www.edsurge.com/news/2017-10-12-udacity-official-declares-moocs-dead-though-the-company-still-offers-them.

7. For a short, book-length treatment of the limits of online education delivery "at scale" as the edtech futurists are fond of touting, see: Jonathan A. Poritz and Jonathan Rees, *Education Is Not an App* (New York: Routledge, 2017).

8. Thomas L. Friedman, "The Professors' Big Stage," *New York Times*, March 5, 2013. http://www.nytimes.com/2013/03/06/opinion/friedman-the-professors-big-stage.html.

9. Amy Ahearn, "The Flip Side of Abysmal MOOC Completion Rates? Discovering the Most Tenacious Learners," *EdSurge*, February 22, 2017. https://www.edsurge.com/news/2017-02-22-the-flip-side-of-abysmal-mooc-completion-rates-discovering-the-most-tenacious-learners.

10. Another consistent feature of edtech hype is the willingness of people with access to elite institutions—who would never consider sending their own children to a school where students interact primarily with screens—to champion those very schools as a route to upward mobility for others. (I learned the alma maters of Friedman's daughters via their wedding announcements in the *New York Times*.)

11. Anant Agarwal, "Online Universities: It's Time for Teachers to

Join the Revolution," *Guardian*, June 15, 2013. https://www.theguardian.com/education/2013/jun/15/university-education-online-mooc.

12. Audrey Watters and Sara Goldrick-Rab, "Techno Fantasies," *Inside Higher Ed*, March 26, 2015. https://www.insidehighered.com/views/2015/03/26/essay-challenging-kevin-careys-new-book-higher-education.

13. Tressie McMillan Cottom, "Intersectionality and Critical Engagement with the Internet," in *The Intersectional Internet: Race, Sex, Class, and Culture Online*. Edited by Safiya Umoja Noble and Brendesha M. Tynes (Vienna: Peter Lang, 2015). https://tressiemc.files.wordpress.com/2012/10/intersectionality-and-critical-engagement-with-the-internet-cottom2.pdf.

14. Jeffrey R. Young, "The New Rock-Star Professor," *Slate*, November 6, 2013. http://www.slate.com/articles/technology/future_tense/2013/11/udacity_coursera_should_celebrities_teach_moocs.html.

15. Bernard Fryshman, "My Yellowing Notes, My Class and Me," *Inside Higher Ed*, February 28, 2014. https://www.insidehighered.com/views/2014/02/28/wonders-traditional-college-classroom-essay.

16. Gallup, "The 2014 Gallup-Purdue Index Report" (2014). http://www.gallup.com/services/176768/2014-gallup-purdue-index-report.aspx.

17. Eric Westervelt, "Meet the Mind-Reading Robo Tutor in the Sky," *Morning Edition*, NPR, October 13, 2015. http://www.npr.org/sections/ed/2015/10/13/437265231/meet-the-mind-reading-robo-tutor-in-the-sky.

18. Bill Gates, "Our Education Efforts Are Evolving," *Gates Notes* (blog), October 19, 2017. https://www.gatesnotes.com/Education/Council-of-Great-City-Schools.

19. Kurt Wagner, "Priscilla Chan Is Running One of the Most Ambitious Philanthropies in the World," *Recode*, July 10, 2017. https://www.recode.net/2017/7/10/15771676/priscilla-chan-facebook-philanthropy-mark-zuckerberg-initiative-cure-diseases.

20. Casey Newton, "Inside Facebook's Plan to Build a Better School," *The Verge*, September 5, 2015. https://www.theverge.com/2015/9/3/9252845/facebook-education-software-plp-summit.

21. John F. Pane, Elizabeth D. Steiner, Matthew D. Baird, Laura S. Hamilton, and Joseph D. Pane, *Informing Progress: Insights on Personalized Learning Implementation and Effects* (Santa Monica, CA: Rand Corporation, 2017). https://www.rand.org/pubs/research_reports/RR2042.html.

22. Benjamin Herold, "The Case(s) Against Personalized Learning," *Education Week*, November 7, 2017. https://www.edweek.org/ew/articles/2017/11/08/the-cases-against-personalized-learning.html.

23. Doug Levin, "Why Do Students in Personalized Learning Programs Feel Less Positive about School?" *EdTech Strategies* (blog), July 13, 2017. https://www.edtechstrategies.com/research-insights/why-do-students-in-personalized-learning-programs-feel-less-positive-about-school/.

24. Adam Satariano, "Silicon Valley Tried to Reinvent Schools. Now It's Rebooting," *Bloomberg Technology*, November 1, 2017. https://www.bloomberg.com/news/articles/2017-11-01/silicon-valley-tried-to-reinvent-schools-now-it-s-rebooting.

25. Jeffrey R. Young, "Hitting Reset, Knewton Tries New Strategy: Competing with Textbook Publishers," *EdSurge*, November 30, 2017. https://www.edsurge.com/news/2017-11-30-hitting-reset-knewton-tries-new-strategy-competing-with-textbook-publishers.

26. The full story of Amplify, and the source for this information, is a chapter in Jonathan A. Knee, *Class Clowns: How the Smartest Investors Lost Billions in Education* (New York: Columbia University Press, 2016), 56–89.

27. Quoted in: Rick Hess, "A Confession and a Question on Personalized Learning," *Education Week* (*Rick Hess Straight Up* blog), February 12, 2018.

28. John Markoff, "Essay-Grading Software Offers Professors a Break," *New York Times*, April 4, 2013. http://www.nytimes.com/2013/04/05/science/new-test-for-computers-grading-essays-at-college-level.html?hp.

29. Steve Kolowich, "Writing Instructor, Skeptical of Automated Grading, Pits Machine vs. Machine," *The Chronicle of Higher Education*, April 28, 2014. http://www.chronicle.com/article/Writing-Instructor-Skeptical/146211.

The Problem of Folklore

1. Richard Braddock, Richard Lloyd-Jones, and Lowell Schoer, *Research in Written Composition* (Urbana, IL: National Council of Teachers of English, 1963), 37–38.

2. National Council of Teachers of English, "Resolution on Grammar Exercises to Teach Speaking and Writing," November 30, 1985. http://www2.ncte.org/statement/grammarexercises/.

3. Lou LaBrant, "Teaching High-School Students to Write," *The English Journal* 35, no. 3 (March 1946): 123.

4. W. B. Elley, *The Role of Grammar in a Secondary School Curriculum*, Educational Research Series No. 60 (Urbana, IL: National Council of Teachers of English, 1979).

5. Michelle Navarre Cleary, "The Wrong Way to Teach Grammar," *The Atlantic*, February 25, 2014. https://www.theatlantic.com/education /archive/2014/02/the-wrong-way-to-teach-grammar/284014/.

6. Joan Didion. https://www.goodreads.com/quotes/915130-grammar -is-a-piano-i-play-by-ear-since-i.

The Problem of Precarity

1. CCCC Executive Committee, "Principles for the Postsecondary Teaching of Writing," March 2015. http://www.ncte.org/cccc/resources /positions/postsecondarywriting#principle11.

2. Susan Schorn, "Teaching in Thin Air," *Inside Higher Ed* (*Just Visiting* blog), October 29, 2014. https://www.insidehighered.com/blogs /just-visiting/guest-post-susan-schorn-teaching-thin-air.

3. Richard H. Haswell, "Average Time-on-Course of a Writing Teacher." http://comppile.org/profresources/compworkload.htm.

4. AAUP, "Trends in the Academic Labor Force 1975–2015," March 2017. https://www.aaup.org/sites/default/files/Academic_Labor _Force_Trends_1975-2015.pdf.

5. Alastair Gee, "Facing Poverty, Academics Turn to Sex Work and Sleeping in Cars," *The Guardian*, September 28, 2017. https://www .theguardian.com/us-news/2017/sep/28/adjunct-professors-homeless -sex-work-academia-poverty.

6. Ken Jacobs, Ian Perry, and Jenifer MacGillvary, "The High Public Cost of Low Wages," UC Berkeley Labor Center Research Brief, April 2015. http://laborcenter.berkeley.edu/pdf/2015/the-high-public-cost -of-low-wages.pdf.

7. Colleen Flaherty, "One Course Without Pay," *Inside Higher Ed,* December 16, 2014. https://www.insidehighered.com/news/2014/12/16 /arizona-state-tells-non-tenure-track-writing-instructors-teach-extra -course-each.

8. "Database: ASU employee salaries," *The State Press.* http://www .statepress.com/article/2017/04/spinvestigative-salary-database.

9. Jenny Anderson, "America Is Slowly Sucking the Life Out of Education—Starting with Its Teachers," *Quartz*, September 12, 2017. https://qz.com/1074113/oecd-2017-report-america-is-slowly-sucking -the-life-out-of-education-starting-with-its-teachers/.

10. Rebecca Klein, "American Teachers Feel Really Stressed, And It's Probably Affecting Students," *Huffington Post*, April 9, 2014. https:// www.huffingtonpost.com/2014/04/09/gallup-education-report_n _5119966.html. This is a summary of Gallup's "State of America's Schools"

report (http://www.gallup.com/services/178709/state-america-schools -report.aspx).

11. Daniel Koretz, *The Testing Charade: Pretending to Make Schools Better* (Chicago: University of Chicago Press, 2017), 2–3.

12. Lyndsey Layton, "Is the Classroom a Stressful Place? Thousands of Teachers Say Yes," *Washington Post*, May 12, 2015. https://www .washingtonpost.com/local/education/is-the-classroom-a-stressful-place -thousands-of-teachers-say-yes/2015/05/12/829f56d8-f81b-11e4-9030 -b4732caefe81_story.html.

13. Leib Sutcher, Linda Darling-Hammond, and Desiree Carver-Thomas, "A Coming Crisis in Teaching? Teacher Supply, Demand, and Shortages in the U.S.," *Learning Policy Institute*, September 2016. https:// learningpolicyinstitute.org/sites/default/files/product-files/A_Coming _Crisis_in_Teaching_REPORT.pdf.

14. Sylvia Allegretto and Lawrence Mishel, "The Teacher Pay Gap Is Wider Than Ever," *Economic Policy Institute*, August 9, 2016. http://www .epi.org/publication/the-teacher-pay-gap-is-wider-than-ever-teachers-pay -continues-to-fall-further-behind-pay-of-comparable-workers/.

15. Anya Kamenetz, "Teachers with Student Debt: The Struggle, The Causes and What Comes Next," NPR, July 16, 2017. http://www .npr.org/sections/ed/2017/07/16/536488351/teachers-with-student-debt -the-struggle-the-causes-and-what-comes-next.

Why School?

1. Ken Bain, *What the Best College Teachers Do* (Cambridge, MA: Harvard University Press, 2004).

2. No Kid Hungry, "Hunger Facts." http://www.nokidhungry.org /who-we-are/hunger-facts.

3. James Dubick, Brandon Mathews, and Clare Cady, "Hunger on Campus: The Challenge of Food Insecurity for College Students," National Student Campaign against Hunger and Homelessness, October 2016. https://studentsagainsthunger.org/hunger-on-campus/.

4. Katharine M. Broton and Sara Goldrick-Rab, "Going Without: An Exploration of Food and Housing Insecurity among Undergraduates," *Educational Researcher*, December 7, 2017. http://journals.sagepub .com/doi/full/10.3102/0013189X17741303.

5. Wendy Troxel, "Why School Should Start Later for Teens," TEDx-ManhattanBeach, November 2016. https://www.ted.com/talks/wendy _troxel_why_school_should_start_later_for_teens/transcript.

6. Christopher Emdin, *For White Folks Who Teach in the Hood . . . and the Rest of Y'all Too* (Boston, MA: Beacon Press, 2016), 33.

7. Emdin, 27.

8. Emdin, 65.

9. The University of Illinois, Virginia Tech, Clemson, College of Charleston.

10. Yep, that really happened. Valerie Strauss, "Kindergarten Show Canceled So Kids Can Keep Studying to Become 'College and Career Ready.' Really." *Washington Post*, April 26, 2014.

11. Peter Greene, "What Is a Child Worth?" *Curmudgucation* (blog), November 10, 2017. http://curmudgucation.blogspot.com/2017/11/what -is-child-worth.html.

12. John Dewey, "My Pedagogic Creed," *School Journal* 54 (January 1897): 77–80. http://dewey.pragmatism.org/creed.htm.

13. Sarah McGrew, Teresa Ortega, Joel Breakstone, and Sam Wineburg, "The Challenge That's Bigger Than Fake News: Civic Reasoning in a Social Media Environment," *American Educator*, Fall 2017. https:// www.aft.org/ae/fall2017/mcgrew_ortega_breakstone_wineburg.

14. Cathy Davidson, "Should We Really ABOLISH the Term Paper? A Response to the NY Times," *HASTAC* (blog), January 21, 2012. https://www.hastac.org/blogs/cathy-davidson/2012/01/21/should-we -really-abolish-term-paper-response-ny-times.

Increasing Rigor

1. In my late twenties I would start playing the drums. For a time I even performed in an indie rock outfit called Quiet Kid, which you could have caught as the opening act of the opening act's opener at one of Chicago's finer rock venues.

2. Mina P. Shaughnessy, *Errors and Expectations: A Guide for the Teacher of Basic Writing* (New York: Oxford University Press, 1979).

Making Writing Meaningful by Making Meaningful Writing

1. Michele Eodice, Anne Ellen Geller, and Neal Lerner, *The Meaningful Writing Project: Learning, Teaching and Writing in Higher Education* (Logan, UT: Utah State University Press, 2017), 4–7.

2. Helen Sword, *Air & Light & Time & Space: How Successful Academics Write* (Cambridge, MA: Harvard University Press, 2017), 4–7.

Writing Experiences

1. The exception to this are people who work in the lab sciences, who often detail their instructions to borderline-absurd levels. I have to tell them to stop writing or it might take the entire period for them to complete the work. They are trained to think of a writing problem in a way

that intersects perfectly with this kind of task, but they can also go over-board with the level of detail. A peanut butter and jelly sandwich does not require the same precision as a laboratory experiment.

2. Daniel T. Willingham, "How to Get Your Mind to Read," *New York Times,* November 25, 2017. https://www.nytimes.com/2017/11/25/opinion/sunday/how-to-get-your-mind-to-read.html?_r=0.

3. Stephen Chew, "How to Get the Most Out of Studying." https://www.youtube.com/watch?v=RH95h36NChI.

4. It bugs me when I go back and read old posts that contain awk-ward bits or even typos, the kinds of things I would mark on student essays. But it also reminds me to focus on what's important for different audiences and occasions. If I had to polish every last word in the blog posts, I would never produce one hundred thousand words a year. The goal is to put ideas into the world, not to impress with my flawless prose each time out.

What about Academics?

1. Richard L. Larson, "The 'Research Paper' in the Writing Course: A Non-Form of Writing," *College English* 44, no. 8 (December 1982): 811–816.

2. Barbara Fister, "Why the 'Research Paper' Isn't Working," *Inside Higher Ed*, April 12, 2011. https://www.insidehighered.com/blogs/library_babel_fish/why_the_research_paper_isn_t_working.

3. Quoted in: Dan Berrett, "Skimming the Surface," *Inside Higher Ed,* April 11, 2011. https://www.insidehighered.com/news/2011/04/11/study_of_first_year_students_research_papers_finds_little_evidence_they_understand_sources.

4. Sandra Jamieson, "What Students' Use of Sources Reveals about Advanced Writing Skills," *Across the Disciplines* 10, no. 3 (December 11, 2013). https://wac.colostate.edu/atd/reading/jamieson.cfm.

5. Paul Thomas, "Real-World Citation versus the Drudgery of Ac-ademic Writing," *Radical Eyes for Equity* (blog), November 28, 2017. https://radicalscholarship.wordpress.com/2017/11/28/real-world-citation-versus-the-drudgery-of-academic-writing/.

What about Grammar?

1. David Foster Wallace, "Shipping Out," *Harper's*, January 1996. 33–56; David Foster Wallace, *A Supposedly Fun Thing I'll Never Do Again* (Boston, MA: Back Bay Books, 1998), 256.

2. *A Supposedly Fun Thing I'll Never Do Again* contains what I think of as the "director's cut" versions of David Foster Wallace's work. In

many cases, the book versions threaten to become excessive, overwhelming the reader with Wallace's stylistic choices, but even this seems deliberate, a desire to test the reader as to how far they're willing to go with him.

What about Grades?

1. Arie W. Kruglanski, Chana Stein, and Aviah Riter, "Contingencies of Exogenous Reward and Task Performance: On the 'Minimax' Strategy in Instrumental Behavior," *Journal of Applied Sociology* 7, no. 2 (June 1977): 141–148.

2. Alfie Koh, "The Case Against Grades," *Educational Leadership* 69, no. 3 (November 2011): 28–33.

3. An important, book-length treatment of academic dishonesty and cheating, including plagiarism, is: James M. Lang, *Cheating Lessons: Learning from Academic Dishonesty* (Cambridge, MA: Harvard University Press, 2013).

4. Arthur Chiaravalli, "Teachers Going Gradeless: Toward a Future of Growth Not Grades," *Teachers Going Gradeless* (blog), April 8, 2017. https://medium.com/teachers-going-gradeless/teachers-going-gradeless-50d621c14cad.

5. Jesse Stommel, "Why I Don't Grade." http://www.jessestommel.com/why-i-dont-grade/.

6. Chiaravalli.

What about the Children?

1. Susan Engel, *The Hungry Mind* (Cambridge, MA: Harvard University Press, 2015).

2. Those weekend news assignments later provided the inspiration for what would become my first published book, *My First Presidentiary: A Scrapbook of George W. Bush* (New York: Crown, 2001). Co-authored by Kevin Guilfoile, it takes the form of a school "primer" helping the new president learn his job. Kevin and I were offered a contract after creating excerpts from George W. Bush's Republican convention "diary"—done exactly in the weekend news style, including crude, colored-pencil drawings.

3. Janet L. Elliott, *Using the Writer's Notebook in Grades 3–8: A Teacher's Guide* (Urbana, IL: National Council of Teachers of English, 2008).

What about the Teachers?

1. Quoted in: Daniel Koretz, *The Testing Charade: Pretending to Make Schools Better* (Chicago: University of Chicago Press, 2017), 200.

2. Koretz, 200.

3. Kenneth Bernstein, "Warnings from the Trenches," *Academe* (AAUP blog), January–February 2013. https://www.aaup.org/article/warnings -trenches#.Wi_fNXeZNAY.

4. Diane Stark Rentner, Nancy Kober, and Matthew Frizzell, *Listen to Us: Teacher Views and Voices* (Washington, DC: Center on Education Policy, May 5, 2016). https://www.cep-dc.org//displayDocument .cfm?DocumentID=1456.

5. Deanna Pan, "South Carolina's Teacher Shortage Nears Crisis, But It's Not All about Money," *Charleston Post and Courier*, February 12, 2018. https://www.postandcourier.com/news/south-carolina-s-teacher -shortage-nears-crisis-but-it-s/article_448aee34-fb9c-11e7-9eb1 -139e6df651d8.html.

6. Pan.

7. Jody Stallings, "Low Pay Not the Main Reason S.C. Facing Teacher Shortage," Opinion, *Charleston Post and Courier*, February 14, 2017. https:// www.postandcourier.com/opinion/commentary/low-pay-not-the-main -reason-s-c-facing-teacher/article_1e49f5d6-11cb-11e8-bca8-b38c2562cc30 .html.

8. "MLA Recommendation on Minimum Per-Course Compensation for Part-Time Faculty Members," May 2017. https://www.mla.org /Resources/Research/Surveys-Reports-and-Other-Documents/Staffing -Salaries-and-Other-Professional-Issues/MLA-Recommendation-on -Minimum-Per-Course-Compensation-for-Part-Time-Faculty -Members.

In Conclusion

1. Karen F. Osterman, "Students' Need for Belonging in the School Community," *Review of Educational Research* 70, no. 3 (Autumn 2000): 323–367.

Index

John Warner is a writer, editor, and college instructor with over twenty years of experience. Since 2012 he has written the "Just Visiting" blog twice weekly for *Inside Higher Ed.*

After receiving both an MA (literature) and MFA (creative writing) from McNeese State University in 1997, he worked as an analyst for Chicago-based marketing research firm Leo J. Shapiro & Associates before returning to teaching in 2001. Since then he has taught writing courses ranging from first-year writing, to fiction writing, to technical writing, to humor writing (and many others), at four different institutions—the University of Illinois, Virginia Tech, Clemson University, and the College of Charleston, where he currently holds the title of faculty affiliate.

His first book, published in 2001 (*My First Presidentiary: A Scrapbook of George W. Bush,* with coauthor Kevin Guilfoile), was written primarily in colored pencil and became a *Washington Post* number one best seller. Since then he has published a parody of writing advice (*Fondling Your Muse: Infallible Advice from a Published Author to a Writerly Aspirant*), more politically minded humor (*So You Want to Be President?*), a novel (*The Funny Man*), and a collection of short stories (*Tough Day for the Army*).

From 2003 to 2008 he edited *McSweeney's Internet Tendency,* for which he now serves as a contributing editor, and since 2012 he has written a weekly column on books and reading as his alter ego, "The Biblioracle," for the *Chicago Tribune.* He is a frequent campus speaker on a variety of topics, including how to survive in the world with an English degree (or three), issues regarding contingent academic labor, how to write for the broader public, humor writing, and of course, writing pedagogy.

In early 2019, a book of writing "experiences" rooted in his approach to teaching writing, *The Writer's Practice: Building Confidence in Your Nonfiction Writing,* will be published by Penguin Random House.

He lives in Mount Pleasant, South Carolina, with his wife, Kathy, and their dogs, Oscar and Truman.